HOW TO AVOID
CATACLYSMS

Tatyana N. Mickushina

UDC 141.339=111=03.161.1
BBC 87.7+86.4

M59 Mickushina, T.N.
HOW TO AVOID CATACLYSMS
The Teaching of the Masters of Wisdom through T. N. Mickushina
2018. – 194 pages

In the years 2005-2012, T. N. Mickushina received with the help of a special technique, Messages from the Lords of Wisdom. This comprehensive and harmonious Teaching deals with all spheres of life for humankind.

In this book, different Masters present Messages and fragments of Messages revealing the Teaching about "How to avoid Cataclysms."

UDC 141.339
BBC 87.7+86.4

ISBN-10: 1729637515
ISBN-13: 978-1729637517

Contents

3

Do not treat your planet as something permanent and given to you once and forever.

Your planet, the state in which it is now, is a reflection of your thoughts, feelings, and the level of consciousness that you have now.

That is why the future of your planet and the climate of your planet and everything that surrounds you on your native planet, your Mother, depends on you and nobody else.

Beloved Alpha
December 14, 2005

Preface

Throughout 2005-2012, I was fortunate enough to receive the Teaching in the form of Messages from the etheric octaves of Light.

Over 50 Beings of Light came to give instructions and training to humanity. They are known in the different ways: The Lords of Wisdom, The Lords of Shambhala, The Great White Brotherhood, The Ascended Masters. Among them are well-known names like: Jesus, Gautama Buddha, Lord Shiva, Mother Mary, Confucius, Zarathustra, and also the less well-known: Elohim Hercules, Elohim Peace, Beloved Alpha, Lord Surya, Athena Pallas, Quan Yin...

The Teaching given by Them covers all the spheres of human life and is not a new Teaching. This Doctrine has existed throughout the development of mankind. The language changed, the countries changed, the Messengers came and went through which the Teaching was given. But the essence of it remained the same, since its Divine Source is the same. The Teaching given through me was published in the series of books "The Words of Wisdom" and on the "Sirius" website.

We can also see certain aspects of this Teaching by collecting separate Messages on specific topics.

In this book, different Masters present Messages and fragments of Messages revealing the Teaching about cataclysms.

Is a global cataclysm threatening the planet?

Is there a connection between the level of consciousness of mankind and such phenomena as extreme weather conditions, earthquakes and volcanic eruptions, wars and revolutions? Can anyone who reads these lines help in ridding the planet of natural and man-made cataclysms, social upheavals and wars? To these and many other questions, the reader will receive the answer, by becoming acquainted with the Words of Wisdom gathered in this book.

Tatyana Mickushina.
Light and Love!

The Earth is living **through a critical time** at present

Sanat Kumara
March 22, 2005

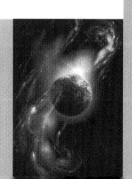

The Earth is living through a critical time at present

Sanat Kumara
March 22, 2005

...

A verbal explanation of the forthcoming events can reflect only a small part of these events and has a very approximate and probabilistic character.

At the very moment when the entire creation was started all the future events were already planned in the form of their probability.

In our world there are such notions as the Zodiac and the signs of the Zodiac. For a person acquainted with the language of stars, all the present and future events are already written down in the information field formed by the manifested stars. If you could master the language of stars perfectly, then you would be able to read the future of your planet written in the universal language of this universe.

But you can hardly find a temporal astrologist capable of understanding this language at present.

The true knowledge that is the key to the language of stars and allows to foresee the future is hidden from contemporary man, just in the same way that you are not permitted to foresee death and know your future and past. This knowledge is also hidden from you.

But the future and the past are determined by the present, by every minute and every second of your present. Time and space limits are actual for your world. There are no such limits in the Higher Worlds. That is why the perfect matrix of creation can manifest itself in space-temporal coordinates in many ways, but the probability of these ways is determined by your every-minute choice.

Therefore, the plan for the universe's evolution, which also includes the plan for your planet, can change within a definite range, but this range is limited by frames. If the evolution of some planet takes place somewhere on the boundary of the channel set up for this planet by the Highest Plan, the whole Hierarchy of Space Beings interferes to correct this evolution when necessary.

It has happened many times with your planet already. The evolution would reach some certain critical point and turn back to the former safe channel.

The danger for evolution appears when it cuts itself off from the Higher Forces and the Hierarchs of the universe, from God and the Divine Law.

There are certain critical points in the history of any planet as well as in the history of Earth. These critical points are determined by the zodiac and its cosmic cycles. At these points we check whether the information field of the Space Law and its direction are in conformity with the direction of the evolution of the lifestreams on the planet. At these moments, the evolution of the planet is corrected when the deflection of the evolution from the direction originally set up exceeds the critical point.

Nowadays, a similar phenomenon takes place. The evolution of the planet has deflected from the trajectory set up by the Space Law, and it requires a correction.

We come recurrently through different prophets and messengers to remind you about the governing Law and the necessity to observe it.

All the predictions of the past and present about the doomsday and different disasters are nothing else but reminders for you about the necessity to obey the Law governing this Universe.

The Law will be observed independently of whether you wish to obey it or not.

The Higher Forces have always taken aim to hold mankind on the edge of the precipice and to restrain it from self-destruction.

We have always helped mankind and we help it now to broaden the consciousness of people, to help them overcome their inner limitations, and to ascend to the next level of the evolution of consciousness.

The Earth is living through a critical time at present. The task that lies before mankind now is to realize the fact that apart from the physical plane there are also Higher planes and that Man is a Great Space Spiritual Being. Man's potential is great.

But mastering this potential will not happen until Man overcomes those traits that are tying him down to the physical plane.

When we watch some of you from the higher plane where we ascended, we sometimes have the same feelings as you have when watching an ant.

14

You may have watched an ant dragging a large burden towards its ant hill. From your level you can better see the path it should take. You see that the path could have been shorter, and the ant hill could have been reached faster and with less force applied.

If you watch an ant, then you will understand the feelings we have when watching your evolution.

In the same way, if you set yourselves to do an ant's job, then we cannot fulfill it for you because your tasks must be performed by you.

We may render certain assistance and we are doing it constantly, but only within the frames permitted by the Law.

One kind of help we give is reminding you of the cosmic deadlines and explaining to you who you are in reality.

Your potential is great. In contradistinction to you, an ant will not be able to achieve a human form of evolution in this manvantara, i.e., this period of the universe's evolution. But you will still be able to manifest your true Divine nature before the end of this manvantara.

That is why we undertake such great efforts to prevent the destruction of the very physical platform, Earth, which has sheltered you and grants you a safe environment for life and development.

Each cataclysm, each natural calamity, is a consequence of your imperfect consciousness. In truth, you reap the fruit of your disobedience, egoism, and obstinacy when you meet face to face with such manifestations of the elements.

The information fields of mankind and of Earth are very closely linked and interwoven.

That is why any imperfect thought exerts influence upon the entire planet, spreading around the globe and coming into resonance with similar imperfect thoughts and feelings.

In the same way, thoughts appealing to Weal and Good — positive thought-forms and emotions — improve the stability of the whole planet and contribute to the leveling of the axis of the equator.

Billions of Space Beings are ready to serve tirelessly day and night to let you exist and evolve in peace, to prevent many of the possible catastrophes and cataclysms, or to soften their effect.

But your help must also be included in the actions of the Ascended Hosts.

Meditate on Good, Weal, and Love. Keep internal peace and quietness. Each of you should become a fulcrum on Earth, a conductor of Light. This Light will help you equalize the balance of your planet. This Light will help Earth in ascending to the next level of evolution.

...

I AM Sanat Kumara.

...*All the disharmonious manifestations in this world are caused by the disharmonious and imperfect consciousness of the earthlings.*

And indeed, everything that takes place and that might take place on planet Earth depends on each of you.

Gautama Buddha
May 23, 2005

Each of your acts of service to all the living creatures reduces the probability of the next threatening cataclysm

Lord of the World
Gautama Buddha,
May 2, 2005

Each of your acts of service to all the living creatures reduces the probability of the next threatening cataclysm

**Lord of the World Gautama Buddha,
May 2, 2005**

...every time natural cataclysms, natural calamities, technogenic catastrophes, wars, terrorist acts, social explosions, or extreme weather conditions occur during this and the following years, let it be a reminder for you about the difficult situation on planet Earth and about the responsibility you bear for the future of this planet.

I am aware of the fact that very many people on planet Earth are unable to understand the link between their actions, thoughts, and feelings and the cataclysms happening on Earth. However, the law governing in this universe extends for this planet as well.

Those of you who have a more advanced consciousness must serve the individuals who have not yet reached the level of comprehension of the close interconnection between everything existing on this planet.

That is why in these Dictations we remind you again and again about your responsibility for your thoughts, feelings, and deeds, for all the actions you perform in your life, for the spending of every erg of the Divine energy.

And, as always, the major part of the work and responsibility for the stabilization of the situation on Earth is laid upon those who possess a higher level of consciousness.

...

Each of your acts of service to a neighbor and service to all living creatures raises the vibrations of planet Earth and reduces the probability of the next threatening cataclysm.

Judge your spiritual progress not by the quantity of hours you have spent in prayers and meditations. Judge your spiritual progress by the help you give to all living creatures, including people, animals and plants. Judge your spiritual progress by those thoughts and feelings that dominate in your consciousness.

These will be the fruit by which Jesus called you to judge.

I take my leave of you.

I AM staying in peace.
Gautama.

I appoint you to be on duty on planet Earth

Beloved Surya,
May 10, 2005

I appoint you to be on duty on planet Earth

Beloved Surya,
May 10, 2005

...Your cities represent accumulations of such amounts of the dark forces that we marvel how you are able to weather these sewers of mass consciousness of this so-called modern civilization.

The sprouts of a new consciousness should pave their way in the silence of nature. In the course of time a new civilization will come to replace the existing one. It will differ from the existing civilization by its harmony of interrelations between man and nature.

And believe me, all the severe climatic conditions and all the extreme weather conditions are just the consequences of your imperfect consciousness.

Do alter your consciousness — I mean the consciousness of humanity as a whole — and the living conditions in your world will change too. And those nature spirits who are now perishing in thousands and literally go mad because of your civilization will soon establish the Divine order on Earth.

The Earth will turn into a planet with such a soft climate and with such perfect living conditions that you will not have to waste so much effort and energy to heat your dwellings.

Look around yourselves. It is you and only you who are responsible for the imperfection of your world. It is you and only you who may be blamed for all the hurricanes, natural calamities, tsunamis and extreme weather conditions. These are the fruits of your hands and your consciousness.

Do not expect the Ascended Hosts to descend and to establish order in your homes. No, beloved. It is your planet, your native home, and you must put it in order by yourselves.

The time has come to clear your consciousness of the debris that has accumulated there during millions of years of your staying in embodiment on planet Earth. Now you must clean your mind and swab your home, your planet Earth.

You are liable for cleaning your planet. I appoint you to be on duty on planet Earth.

I AM Surya.

Try to keep the state
of inner peace and
harmony during most
of the day

Beloved Kuthumi
May 19, 2005

Try to keep the state of inner peace and harmony during most of the day

Beloved Kuthumi
May 19, 2005

I AM Kuthumi, having come to you again. I have come today to give you a small Teaching which perhaps may seem unexpected to you, but I would still like you to carefully familiarize yourselves with everything that I consider necessary to bring to your consciousness at this stage.

As you know, the event that took place at the end of last year — an earthquake and a tsunami — was entirely caused by the imperfect consciousness of mankind.

With surprising persistence, humanity continues to give birth to monstrous masses of negative energies that have wrapped the entire globe with a thick envelope. This envelope prevents the penetration of the renewal energies. In other words, a tension has been created between the forces that strive to keep the existing state on the planet and the forces striving to contribute to the implementation of the evolutionary plan for planet Earth.

On the one hand, you witness the constant and steady rise of the vibrations of the planet. On the other hand, an enormous amount of negative energy is still produced with the help of mass consciousness and the old stereotypes deeply ingrained in the consciousness of people. Where does the negative energy come from?

All the energy in this Universe is concentrated in only one source, and that is the Divine energy. This energy comes to you along the crystal string, and you use this energy of your own free will. If you waste this energy to satisfy any of your egoistic strivings or to maintain negative thoughts, qualities, or persistent bad habits, then it means that you vote for the obsolete way of living. You direct your energy to strengthen the masses of negative energy on this planet.

Therefore, when the positive energy of change meets with the negative energy produced by humanity, it is like a clash of two clouds with different charges. You know what happens when such clouds collide. You can observe thunder and lightning. Something similar is taking place on planet Earth at present. When two masses of energies with opposite potential clash, various disasters happen — for example, natural calamities and hurricanes.

It may seem to you that the natural elements are blind and uncontrollable. However, this is not quite true. As a rule, we manage to localize the masses of emerging negative energy at the places where they appear. That is why the areas that contribute to the production of the negative energetic masses with their consciousness suffer from the natural calamities.

Beloved, it is time to part with the point of view that you can commit sins, act in improper ways, think and feel in ways unpleasing to God during most of the day, and then after that you can sit down, pray, and transmute the karma that you and your loved ones have created.

There is no doubt that the benefits of prayers are unquestionable, undeniable, and indisputable. The effectiveness of prayers is beyond discussion. But it is not enough just to pray in this situation, beloved.

What is the point of first producing negative energetic masses and then fighting against them?

It is time for you to approach everything you do during the day consciously. You should constantly control your thoughts and feelings. Any negative thought in your consciousness must be nipped in the bud. Protect yourself from everything that contributes to the existence of negative thoughts and feelings in your consciousness.

Pay special attention to your children. Do not leave them alone during most of the day. Remember that the fruit that you will get literally in a few years will depend on the direction you show your children at the beginning of their lives and on the knowledge that you give them about the laws operating in this Universe, for your children will grow up and will be able to take responsibilities upon themselves and to serve for the benefit of the evolution of Earth. Each of you is responsible for the future of this planet and for the unfolding of the events in the coming months.

Remember that the tension, which was defused by the cataclysm in the south of Asia at the end of last year, is increasing again. As a matter of fact, with every negative action and every negative thought and feeling, you tirelessly draw a new cataclysm nearer.

Try to keep the state of inner peace and harmony during most of the day. Do not forget that other people live next to you. If you live in a big city, during the day your aura comes into contact with the auras of thousands of people. When you manage to keep a harmonious state within yourself, you literally infect with this state thousands of people with whose auras you come into contact during the day.

Exactly the same effect occurs when you meet a person who is like a thundercloud and seeking someone to ease his tension and to vent his anger. But in this case you are infected with the negative energies of this person.

Protect your inner world against the intrusion of negative energies. Take special care of your children.

You can say that nothing depends on you and that your government is to be blamed for everything because it does not take proper care of you and does not allow you to enjoy a decent way of life.

Allow me to disagree with you. All things in this world are drawn to each other by their vibrations, and you have exactly the government that can exist only because the majority of the population considers it possible to tolerate this government and its policies.

You constantly exchange energies with thousands of people, and thus you constantly exchange karma with them. How do you think the karma of a family is manifested, the karma of the city, the karma of the country, or the planetary karma? Imagine a person who is completely free from his personal karma. What do you think will happen to this person next? Will he ascend?

It is quite probable that such a person can ascend. But let me assure you that a person who has become free from his personal karma acquires a completely different expanded consciousness. He rises up to another higher level in his consciousness and understands that it is impossible to save only his own soul. Actually, everything is God, and at this new level of consciousness the person feels the unity of all the living much more deeply. Such a person is most likely to stay in embodiment regardless of whether his external consciousness is aware of his decision or not. Such a person continues to live in the world of his choice. Every day he draws the negative energies of the people around him into his aura and transmutes these energies. Such a person is like a sponge. As soon as he comes in contact with the auras of people saturated with too much negative energy, he takes a part of this energy upon himself and neutralizes it. A phenomenon occurs that you call the transmutation of the karma of a city, a country, or a planet.

Therefore, very much depends on each of you, beloved, on your ability to keep harmony and balance, in spite of any surrounding circumstances. If you feel depression, lack of joy, causeless melancholy, then it means that you have most likely come under the influence of a large mass of negative energy. You have loaded your aura so heavily that you will need some time to be alone or in nature to restore your inner peace and balance.

Learn to recognize your inner state and the reasons for disharmony in your consciousness.

When you reach a certain level of consciousness that allows you to take upon yourself the karma of a city, a country, or the planet and to transmute this karma, you serve constantly, 24 hours a day.

This is a vital service, beloved. Today I have given these recommendations for you in the hope of explaining the mechanism of such a service to those of you who are already providing this vital service to the world.

And when you are now aware of your service, you will be able to take timely measures for the restoration of your vibrations and energies. Listen carefully to your body, and when you are overcome with depression, find a way to restore your inner harmony and peace. For some of you it can be meditation; for others it can be a prayer, a stroll in nature, listening to relaxing music, or playing with children.

Do not allow yourself to be in the negative state of consciousness for a long time. Suppress all the negative vibrations within you as soon as they arise. Do not let them take hold of your being.

And remember that you always have an opportunity to ask the Ascended Hosts for help as a last resort. We will render to our devoted servants all the help that the Cosmic Law will allow us.

I AM Kuthumi, your brother.

Our task is to
impregnate Earth
with the new
vibrations, the new
consciousness, and
the new attitude to
the world

Gautama Buddha
May 23, 2005

Our task is to impregnate Earth with the new vibrations, the new consciousness, and the new attitude to the world

Gautama Buddha
May 23, 2005

I AM Gautama Buddha, having come again.

...

The preventions are being given and the promptings are being sent through different people as it was in the days of Noah. But people prefer to pay no heed and to close their eyes to them, to hear and see nothing.

Some people show wonders of complete irresponsibility and a lack of system, others show wonders of heroism and self-sacrifice, trying to prevent the unavoidable.

Everyone acts the way he prefers to act. And everyone acts depending on whose advice he prefers to follow in his life.

The approaching events will yet again reveal the lack of correspondence between the vibrations of the majority of mankind and the New Age's vibrations that have already reached and are reaching Earth now.

In this way, by following the path of successive approximations, the conceived plan will be realized on planet Earth. My beloved chelas, you should never go against the Will of God, never act in defiance of the plans envisaged by the Supreme Law for planet Earth.

In this way the true aspirations and God-qualities are being cultivated within everyone. Everyone obtains an opportunity to manifest his or her inner essence.

Why are you given a Teaching that says that you should take care only of yourself, your thoughts and feelings? Why cannot you lead other individuals and make them act in the way you think to be right?

This is because everything that happens and is to happen on the planet and with every individual is determined by the presence of these or those energies within people's auras and force fields.

If you have accumulated a great amount of negative energy during many embodiments on Earth and continue keeping this energy, you will not manage to escape the events connected with your karma, irrespective of whatever endeavors you make. On the other hand, if you have taken care of your thoughts and feelings in advance, if you have gotten rid of a major portion of your karmic loads, nobody will be able to harm you in spite of all his attempts.

Your enemies will make every endeavor to harm you. But if there is nothing to catch hold of in your aura, none of their actions will harm you but on the contrary, all their actions will be of benefit to you.

This is the hidden mechanism of surviving in the conditions that are impossible for existence. This explains why some things happen to some people but at the same time do not affect others around them.

Therefore, it is absolutely pointless to waste efforts proving to yourself and to the people around you that you are good and fully devoted to God. All your actions, thoughts, and feelings are kept in your aura and in the so-called Akasha chronicles. Therefore, it is absolutely ridiculous to play any games with the Cosmic Law governing in this universe. That is why it is said that you should take care only of your thoughts and feelings, of your own actions and of what you do.

You cannot help a person if he does not want to accept your help. You cannot force anybody to share your views. But you always have a chance to share the treasures of your knowledge with those who are ready to listen to you. The secret here lies not just in the fact that a person who is ready to accept your care and knowledge has the consciousness and vibrations enabling him to do so, he has obtained this consciousness and these vibrations during not just one of his embodiments.

Therefore, spare no efforts to thrust your views on those who do not want to listen to you. It would be better for you to find people from your environment who are sick and tired of the irreparability of this world and of the stagnant atmosphere they live in. The knowledge you will offer to those people will be a miraculous balm, relieving their existence and salving the wounds they have received when coming into contact with the sides of your world that are not the best.

You always have a chance to find at least one person from your environment who needs your help and the knowledge you can offer. Unfortunately, the level of consciousness of mankind is so low that only the minority of humanity is able to master the knowledge, the energies and the information contained in the Dictations that we are giving now through our Messenger.

We are fully aware of our probable opportunity to awaken the consciousness of only a few thousand or a few tens of thousands of people all over the world.

But believe me, my beloved chelas, it is quite enough for a start.

And that information, and those vibrations, and that knowledge which can be absorbed by those few who have prepared their temples for receiving that information in advance, will be stored in the energy fields of those, in their auras.

The people of Earth are tightly interconnected in the higher plane. There is a conception of the collective unconscious of mankind — when the knowledge that we succeed in putting into the head of one or two men is spread unbeknown to the consciousness of the majority of people. And if they hear somewhere about some knowledge that is completely new for Earth, many of them will have a feeling that they have already heard or known about it, but scarcely will they manage to designate the source from which they have picked up this knowledge.

The high vibrations of our world are capable of reaching many individuals even if there is no feedback in their external consciousness at first. Remember that the construction of a human is like a matryoshka[3] and that

---

[3] A matryoshka doll or a Russian nested doll, also called a stacking doll or Babushka doll, is a set.

the Higher Self of a human is always very responsive to everything that takes place in the informational field of Earth...

... All the disharmonious manifestations in this world are caused by the disharmonious and imperfect consciousness of the earthlings. And indeed, everything that takes place and that might take place on planet Earth depends on each of you. You simply read these Dictations, you simply master the information contained in them. But your influence on the future events on Earth will be like that of a vehicle's spring. You will be able to mitigate every calamity, every cataclysm.

Our task is to impregnate Earth with the new vibrations, the new consciousness and the new attitude to the world through the consciousness of the people who are able to take the knowledge that we give.

Very soon you will see as everything starts changing around you. This will truly resemble a miracle, but this miracle, beloved, will happen only with your help.

I AM Gautama Buddha.

With more refinement taking place on the planet, your thoughts and feelings gain larger influences — a much larger influence than your words and actions.

Prudence and caution are the qualities that you have to acquire. But you acquire these qualities automatically if devotion to the Will of God and a desire to serve your neighbor based on the feeling of unconditional Love are present inside of you.

Beloved Alpha
December 29, 2009

Each of you affects the situation on planet Earth

Beloved Lanello
June 26, 2005

Each of you affects the situation on planet Earth

Beloved Lanello
June 26, 2005

...

I have come to help you become familiarized with my thoughts and views on the present state of things. This relates both to the planet and the country in whose language we give these Dictations.

The present situation in the world does not seem to prognosticate anything unexpected. However, hidden processes are going on in the entrails of the Earth and gradually manifest themselves in the form of volcanic activity and different cataclysms.

The connection between the state of the earth's crust and the level of human consciousness is very strong. You can judge the tension accumulated in the higher plane closest to the Earth by the number of the earth shocks and earthquakes and by their strength and frequency.

The Earth is very sensitive to everything that happens in the human consciousness and in the collective consciousness of humanity.

We can regard our planet Earth as a mother's body that is universal for all the evolutions inhabiting it. In exactly the same way as a mother always senses dangerous situations into which her children can get, even at a considerable distance, Earth reacts to the dangerous states of consciousness of her children. In order to make the analogy complete, you can imagine Mother Earth starting to become distressed for her unwise children when they let serious distortions appear within their consciousness in the form of imperfect thoughts and feelings. Just like any other mother, Mother Earth starts worrying and being distressed for her children, and this is expressed in the increase of the underground activity.

That is why the more people keep their high level of consciousness and send their Love and gratitude to Mother Earth, the more tranquil will be the inevitable changes of the configuration of the continents and oceans existing on the surface of the Earth now.

Every new race that comes to Earth must receive a new continent for its evolution and prosperity.

You should realize that the age is now coming when the new Sixth Root Race is coming into embodiment on Earth. At present, this Race is located on the existing continents but in the future, when the influence of this Race on the evolution of the Earth becomes dominant, it will receive its own continent that will be brought into the world by Earth at the place of one of the present oceans. Correspondingly, old continents such as Europe, a part of Asia, and both Americas will gradually submerge together with the towns and the people inhabiting them.

This process can be gradual and painless and take thousands and tens of thousands of years, but it can also happen almost instantaneously, just as happened when Atlantis went under water with the traces of the Fourth Root Race, the behavior of which resulted in the fact that the catastrophe took on a global character. Actually the entire continent, its largest part, went under water in a few days. It was impossible to escape during the time limit granted by nature, even in spite of the fact that this race had exceptionable ships and flying machines.

The entire deliverance lies only in the level of your consciousness. If your consciousness is on a high enough level to enable you to have a connection with the Ascended Hosts, you will be warned about the future catastrophes beforehand and will have a chance to build your Noah's ark and undertake your exodus to the new lands.

Therefore, if the level of mass consciousness of humanity is able to rise to a higher stage in the near future, the inevitable cataclysms will take place gradually and painlessly and will last for a considerable period of time. But if humanity prefers to go on experimenting with its free will and does not heed the voice of the Divine reason, the character of the cataclysm will be more ruthless and destructive. It is nothing for Earth, when she becomes agitated because of her children, to send a whole continent such as Europe to the bottom of the sea in 24 hours.

I understand that it is difficult for you to believe in the danger that threatens you because you have not experienced anything like that during your lives. The memory of mankind keeps the legends about the drowning of Atlantis, together with the hundreds of thousands of people inhabiting it, as something excessively fantastic to believe in.

When you reach a certain stage in your consciousness, this stage allows you to realize the reality of these legends, and you will even be able to remember your embodiments on the Atlantean continent. And if in the past you were sent to the bottom together with your continent, you would still experience the states of fear and unconscious anxiety during any earthquakes that you would have to live through in your current life. If at the time of Atlantis you happened to be among the people who heeded the voice of the prophets and left the submerged land in advance, it is likely that now you belong to the people who pay close heed to the voices of all the prophets and try to pay attention to the warnings coming through them in your lives.

If we tell you beforehand what can happen on planet Earth in the near future, this may cause panic among the people who remember well that prophecies are sometimes fulfilled. However, any panic is a non-divine manifestation and will result in even greater troubles for the Earth. That is why in the prophecies made for a mainstream audience, nothing definite is ever told about the place and the effective damage risk level of a forthcoming catastrophe.

There are people who are able to identify a serious warning even in a very subtle hint and to begin their prayer practice on neutralizing the negative energy from the collection of thoughts and feelings of earthly mankind, the accumulation of which has become threatening. These people are also trying to ease the anxiety of Mother Earth with the help of Love emitting from their hearts straight into the heart of Mother Earth.

It often happens that the efforts of these people are enough to either prevent the cataclysm completely or alleviate its consequences to the minimum manifestation.

I can add to the above only that each of you affects the situation on planet Earth.

You do not even need to pray but just stop the flow of negative energy in your consciousness, close negative spirals inside your heart, and transform them into rose petals with the help of your heart's Love.

During the day you are constantly watching situations that make Mother Earth worry. Mentally try to take such a situation into your heart and transmute its consequences. Do not condemn the people who create negative manifestations around them and take part in them. Their consciousness is darkened and they are not able yet to realize the harm they are doing to Earth and first of all to themselves. Let God and the Cosmic Law teach these people to obey the Divine Law. If you become an eyewitness to a negative destructive situation, your task is to try to take upon yourself the transmutation of the negative energy that accumulates in the physical, astral, and mental planes because of the wrong actions of other people. They do not know what they are doing, but you know. Thus, do not add extra negative energy into the common muddy stream with your condemnation. Do not feed imperfection with your energy. Just withdraw all the energy from imperfection and try to transmute the created negative energy with the help of your chakras or prayers. Believe me, you will obtain a much better result in this case than if you lecture an uncontrollable and unruly child of Earth.

The prophecy has been pronounced, and God forbid it to be fulfilled.

I AM Lanello.

I come in order to ask you for the help
that your ill planet needs

Beloved Alpha
December 14, 2005

I come in order to ask you for the help that your ill planet needs

Beloved Alpha
December 14, 2005

…Your native planet needs your care and guardianship. Imagine that Earth is your Mother, and your Mother is sick and needs your help.

If you are loving children, then you must respond to your Mother's calling no matter how carried away you are with your life's problems, or how hard it is for you. Because this is your Mother, and she is sick and she needs your help.

The reason I have come to you today is to call you to your Mother and tell you that she needs your help and your care, and your guardianship now as never before.

You have reached the age when you can assume the responsibility for your Mother who is now in need of your help.

There was a time when you were getting help from your Mother. There was a time when you were getting everything you needed: food, heat, care.

Now the time has come to pay your dues, to thank your Mother — your native planet — for everything she has done for you.

Your Mother has a lot of children. And not all of her children are able to respond to the call. For they have lost the connection with their parental home. For they have chosen a path that leads nowhere.

Those of you who can hear me and are able to perceive my vibrations, you will not leave your Mother in trouble.

Can I count on you? Can I? That is why I come, in order to ask you for the help that your sick planet needs now as never before.

You know that the illness of your planet is related to the consequences of those thoughts, feelings, and deeds that the children of Earth admit. You know that your Mother Earth worries about her unwise children. And that is why she is sick. That is why you must give Mother Earth the help that she needs. And she needs your Love. There is no more valuable medicine that you could offer your Mother than the Love of your hearts.

Please, make it a rule, starting from this day, to spare at least several minutes a day to send Love to your native planet. Please remind yourself of the best minutes you have spent in nature, in the mountains, at the river, in the forest. Remember the minutes of joy you have been experiencing from communicating with nature.

Remember quiet summer days and evenings. Remember sunrises and sunsets.

Remember a clear hot summer day and a cool evening. Remember everything that is connected with your best memories.

Thank your Mother Earth for everything that she has given to you in the past. And now, if you can send Love to your Mother, she will be able to recover her health and her life forces, and become a shelter and a sanctuary for many generations of people.

Do not treat your planet as something permanent and given to you once and forever. Your planet, the state in which it is now, is a reflection of your thoughts, feelings, and the level of consciousness that you have now.

That is why the future of your planet and the climate of your planet and everything that surrounds you on your native planet, your Mother, depends on you and nobody else.

I have come to give you a clear understanding that Earth needs your help. And now you know how to provide this help.

I have come to remind you of your duty; and I have come to say that the time to carry out your duty has come. The Cosmic opportunity is not exhausted yet. But you must be continuously feeling your responsibility for everything that surrounds you.

For everything around you was created with your consciousness. And along with the rise of the level of your consciousness, the illusory reality surrounding you will be changed because it will become more Divine, closer to the Divine reality.

I have come. And I have said.

I AM Alpha,
your Father in Heaven. Om.

...any imperfect thought exerts influence upon the entire planet, spreading around the globe and coming into resonance with similar imperfect thoughts and feelings.

In the same way, thoughts appealing to Weal and Good — positive thought-forms and emotions — improve the stability of the whole planet and contribute to the leveling of the axis of the equator.

Sanat Kumara
March 22, 2005

A Teaching on prophets and prophecies

John the Beloved
July 13, 2006

A Teaching on prophets and prophecies

John the Beloved
July 13, 2006

I AM John the Beloved. I am known to you as the author of the Apocalypse. I have come again in order to give a Teaching based on the internal knowledge — the knowledge that was accessible only to prophets and mystics. Such people still exist in your time, but they are often mistaken for charlatans who declare themselves as prophets, clairvoyants, or psychics but the threshold of their perception of the Divine World is not high that at times, it would be better for their future if they stopped their prophecies and became silent.

What do you think — is there any karma carried by prophets, and what is that karma? I will tell you, since I know very well what kind of karma we are talking about.

There is no difference between prophesying and any other activity that you can be engaged in, in the physical world. There are different kinds of prophets. There are prophets making prophecies from the Light, and there are prophets who prophesy from the darkness. Each prophet chooses for himself which forces to serve.

Prophecy is the gift of contact with the invisible world. This gift is not acquired during just one embodiment When this gift is granted, a person prophesying from God usually realizes the full karmic responsibility that rests on his shoulders. Prophecies represent probabilities of the occurrence of events sensed from the subtle plane. Depending on the plane and the level at which the prophecy is sensed, it can be more or less accurate. But because things that are familiar on the physical plane are missing in the Higher world, the gift of prophecy involves interpretation of events based on impressions from contact with the subtle plane.

Since the human mind is involved in the process of the representation of impressions, a distortion of information takes place at this stage, and the authenticity of the prophecy is lost. Since I wrote the Apocalypse with symbols, I managed to avoid the karma that is laid on the Prophet, if the prophecy did not come true. And each prophet who achieved a high level of development provides his veiled knowledge in the form of verses, parables, and quatrains. This is very fair because it makes it possible to avoid karma if the prophecy is erroneous.

There are other prophets who use human interest in prophecies, and give their prophecies in simple language, based on the knowledge they draw from the lowest levels of the astral plane, or while being under the effect of mind-altering drugs.

These prophecies do not contain big truths. And usually they do not come true. The probability of such prophecies coming true is fifty percent. This is the case when people say, "There's many a slip between the cup and the lip."

However, the desire to satisfy human interest in soothsaying puts a great karmic responsibility upon such prophets and clairvoyants. In the case where the prophecy is incorrect, the more people who know about this prophecy, the greater the responsibility is. The fact is that any prophecy programs the consciousness of people who perceive it. And if there are many people who wish to believe the prophecy, then these people create by their consciousness an opportunity for the realization of such a prophecy. And if a phenomenon predicted by a forecaster does not coincide with the Divine vision, but is realized due to the momentum of human consciousness involved in this phenomenon, and if this phenomenon took place, then karma lies upon both the forecaster and the people who contribute to the realization of this phenomenon through their consciousness.

Therefore, any prophecy is a double-edged sword. If a prophecy alters the Divine plane for the better, then the realization of such a prophecy brings good karma to all the people who take part in its realization through their consciousness. If the Divine plane is worsened as a result of the prophecy, then a negative karma is created from the prophecy.

Prophecy is a phenomenon as dual as everything else in your world.

The people who come under the influence of the energy of prophecies of false foretellers create negative karma.

The prophets of Light have always been out of favor because the majority of people did not like the prophecies coming through them. People have always treated such prophets cautiously. They would rather have no dealings with them, and even tried to physically destroy them. The karma of reprisal for actions against a prophet of Light falls as a heavy burden on the next generation.

In contrast, any veneration of God's prophets brought good karma to the family of the person who showed hospitality to a prophet.

True prophets were always Messengers of God, and their mission was necessary in order to contribute to the proper development of human consciousness. Those who declared themselves as prophets without having been stamped with the seal of God incurred a heavy karma descending onto themselves. Therefore, always observe and examine, and do not get involved in any activity relating to prophecies if it is not from God, if it is demonic.

Although hundreds of years have passed since my incarnation, I am giving you this Teaching because it has not lost its relevance. On the contrary, it has acquired urgency since many visionaries and clairvoyants have appeared who do far more harm than good. And if you are involved in their activity, hire them, and pay for their services, then you create karma from a wrong action.

I have come to give you this important Teaching on the true and false prophets in order for you to be able to approach everything you meet on your Path, in this sphere, with your eyes open in your consciousness.

It is very important where you direct your energy. None of the false prophets would be able to foretell if you did not give them the energy of your attention and your money, thus encouraging them to take up this ungodly business.

False prophets are the children of impure human consciousness, ignorance, and superstition.

Now that the major part of the Teaching has been given, I would like to make a prophecy relating to your future. Before my coming to you, the other Ascended Masters and I were pondering whether it was worth giving you this prophecy through this Messenger, because we had to consider the purity of the conductors and the degree of distortion of the information that might occur. We have decided to run a risk, and I will proceed.

In this difficult time in which you are living, you constantly think about many things and especially about the future of your planet, whether there is a threat of the next global cataclysm on it. That is why it is very important for you to hear that no global cataclysm is foreseen during the lifetime of the generation living now. However, everything can change if you do not endeavor to transform your consciousness daily. The stable balance on the planet that has been achieved so far exists and depends on the fact that many people have raised their consciousness to such a level that they are able to think positively and direct their efforts to the Common Wealth, Good, and the Light. If the number of such people increases with each year, no global cataclysm will occur during the life of the next generation either, because each preceding generation paves the way for the next one. Through your consciousness you are preparing a sustainable development for all life on planet Earth, during the next cosmic cycle.

I wish you to just as successfully continue keeping your consciousness at the highest level.

I AM John the Beloved,
with great respect to your lifestreams I AM.

I have come to
affirm the qualities
of joy, aspiration,
and victory in your
consciousness

Lord Maitreya,
October 9, 2006

I have come to affirm the qualities of joy, aspiration, and victory in your consciousness

Lord Maitreya,
October 9, 2006

...

I am happy that we have succeeded in passing the Divine Truth to such a large number of human individuals incarnated in this difficult far-reaching time. And I am happy that many of you have awakened from your long dormancy, which you have been in for more than one incarnation. The time has surely come, and the cosmic opportunity predicted by the prophets of the past has opened up for Earth. It will not take long for this opportunity to appear in the manifested world. Observe all the circumstances that are changing around you. Do not stop mentioning the changes taking place in your diaries. There have never ever been such miracles, which are becoming more and more evident now. I will not be surprised if soon the governments of many countries of the world base the policies of their countries in accordance with the Cosmic Law. They simply will not be able to manage in the old way using old governance techniques, because the consciousness of the masses has changed and demands that all authority institutions adjust to the transformed people's consciousness.

The generation that is coming into life now needs special care and protection. It is exactly this generation that is to fulfill the Divine Plan in the near foreseeable future. Do not be afraid of the changes in your lives or in the situation in the world. Nothing can threaten you if you behave in a proper way and keep the Law properly. None of the disasters or cataclysms can threaten those who faithfully serve God, who exists within all of Life and in each particle of Life.

I have been glad to express my own delight in this Message and to give credit for your efforts, which you apply every day.

And now I would like to give one more little piece of information; this information concerns the events of the so-called Transition that many people are waiting for and preparing themselves for. One should never take any prophecy or any upcoming disaster too seriously because many prophecies were uttered but did not come true, whereas other prophecies that were not uttered did come true. I recommend that you tune in to the present and catch every moment of your life as the one having value for centuries. In fact, nothing exists in the Divine world but eternal "now." And this "now" you create by your own consciousness. One should never pay too much attention to what has already happened or to what has not happened yet. Your mood in every moment of your life is the only thing that forms the future that is waiting for you. Therefore, focus on filling each moment of your life with joy, love, warmth, and happiness because you yourselves are the creators of your happiness, and you yourselves are the creators of your future.

We come to give the Teaching, but you and only you can carry out the changes on your planet when you take in this Teaching and become a bearer of this Teaching for millions of those who have not awakened yet.

I am glad that the time of awakening is coming for many people, and I am glad that I can come so easily and share my state and my mood with you. I will be much happier if I manage to pass my state on to as many incarnated people as possible.

I have been happy with our new meeting, and as always, it is a bit of a pity to part.

See you later, dear friends!

I AM Maitreya!

A more balanced and successful development and your entry into the period of the *Golden Age* are created by the vectors of the consciousness of positively directed individuals.

The more human individuals there are who are able to balance themselves, the surrounding people and conditions, and the greater efforts and aspirations they demonstrate, the sooner humankind will enter the passage of sustainable and stable development.

Beloved Quan Yin
June 24, 2011

Recommendations
to humankind of Earth

Beloved Surya,
June 21, 2007

Recommendations to humankind of Earth

Beloved Surya,
June 21, 2007

I AM Surya, having come to you again from the Great Central Sun. I have come again to humankind of Earth in order to give instructions and to strengthen and develop the connection between the worlds. As usual, I would like to pay attention to the news concerning current events that are revealed now and are taking place in your world and are going to descend into your world in the nearest future because in the finer plane these events are ready to descend into the physical world.

You know that we work with humankind of Earth thanks to the Divine mercy, the dispensation that allows us to correct the course of evolution on the planet. And you know that millions of years ago humanity of Earth deviated from the evolutionary path; and it brought some turmoil to the common course of evolution. Many life-streams got a deceleration of their development, and on the contrary, many life-streams accelerated their development thanks to Divine mercies and opportunities. Each of you can make his or her own choice whether to follow the Divine Law or to continue living in accordance with the laws that have formed on planet Earth and which at the given moment do not quite conform to the plan for the planet, the plan that exists on the Divine level, which should be realized soon.

Please, do understand that we do not wish to cause you pain and suffering. Millions of beings of Light from all over the cosmos are ready to help you. However, you and only you slow down the evolution of the planet. You allow yourselves to perform such deeds and to have such imperfect states of consciousness that are inadmissible at your stage of evolution. We are forced to resort to such measures when literally before your eyes your imperfect deeds, thoughts, and feelings are materialized into outer conditions like unfavorable weather, cataclysms, and troubles that you face in your lives: diseases, afflictions, and misfortunes.

You yourselves are the cause of what happens with you and around you. We all are closely connected in the etheric plane, and we all belong to the common chain of evolutions in the universe. There is no particular difference between you and me. I stand several hundred steps higher than you. And that is the difference between us. Therefore, you should listen to the advice coming from me or from any other Ascended Master who gives his Messages through our representative on Earth, our Messenger Tatyana.

Now you have this opportunity of almost direct communication. Use this opportunity and try to treat our Dictations not as fairy tales you listened to in your childhood before going to bed, but rather, try to treat our Dictations as the guidance that you should follow in your life. Believe me; the opportunity that you have now gives you a great advantage. In such a way we are intending to pull out of the nets of illusion millions of life-streams, lost souls who were wandering about in the thicket of illusion from incarnation to incarnation and who face whole swarms of fears, doubts, misfortunes, and diseases.

We throw our nets again to pull out thousands and millions of lost souls from the waters of the astral plane.

We come in order to give you an impulse, that energy impulse that will allow you to wake up and to turn your eyes to the Heavens, to the bright sun of the New Day, the dawn of the Day that has already begun.

I have come to you today in order to give necessary instructions for the future. You are the beings of Light who are lost in the thicket of the matter, and we give you a helping hand. Please, do not refuse our help, do not show arrogance that is more typical of teenagers, and do listen to our advice.

Due to the Law of Free Will acting in the Universe, you have an opportunity to choose your future yourselves. You have an opportunity to listen to my and our advice, and you have an opportunity to refuse the outstretched helping hand.

I must warn you that now you are hanging over an abyss, and if the mist around you hides this from your view and does not allow you to see your lamentable state, it does not mean there is no danger of rolling down into that abyss at any moment.

You may not believe me. You may continue to stubbornly refuse the offered help. That is your right. But there are individuals among you who ask us for help, and we cannot but help them as the call forces us to respond. We cannot save you by force, but our duty is to offer a helping hand to those who need it.

We are with you for your whole long Path from the matter back to the Divine world. We are with you all along your Path. And very soon, if you follow our advice, you will be able to distinguish us and will consciously receive our assistance. But now you need to believe our Messages and the information that we are giving through our Messenger.

There were always the people who declared themselves Messengers of Heavens. And they spoke on behalf of God. There were people who listened to and followed the advice coming from above, and there were people who mocked at it and followed their own way.

It is your choice. It is your free will.

My task and our tasks are just to warn you about the consequences of your choice. And my task and our tasks are to point out for you that the time has accelerated, and the consequences of your wrong choices will be visible to you in just a couple of days after you have made the wrong choice. This is done especially for you to track with your external consciousness the effect of the Great Cosmic Law of this universe, which in former times was stated in the following way: "As you sow, you shall reap."

It is a very rational Law, the Law-Teacher that helps you learn the mistakes you made in the past. This is

Law that you should learn in schools. The generation, starting their life now, must know this Law. And if there are problems with the introduction of the subject Laws of the Universe at school, you can always explain the effect of this Law to your children and grandchildren. And the more people are informed about this Law, the better the situation on planet Earth will be, as those people who know this Law will beware of breaking it, not because of fear but because of the wish to avoid unnecessary obstacles on their Path.

Believe me, sometimes it is better to get around an obstacle than to climb up a vertical rock without a safety rope.

We come in order to give you our short guidance. Please inform your children and grandchildren about the safety rules of living on planet Earth.

I sincerely hope for your help and support.

I AM Surya,
with all my Love toward you.

The feast of life is over. The time has come for hard inner work.

By unfettering yourselves from low states of consciousness, you save the whole world. This is because everything is interconnected in our worlds.

And a beat of a butterfly's wing is heard as thunder in the subtle worlds. What, then, is the effect of your actions, thoughts, and feelings?

Beloved Quan Yin
June 24, 2011

A Teaching on responsibility to the evolutions of planet Earth

Lord Surya,
December 22, 2007

A Teaching on responsibility to the evolutions of planet Earth

Lord Surya,
December 22, 2007

...

You see that the situation on Earth is changing. You see it with your physical eyes, and you hear it from the radio and TV news.

It is not easy to keep to a path to change the planet and at the same time to balance all the different kinds of energies generated by the collective human consciousness. The situation is that it literally depends on each of you how the process of changing will happen. Earth, as well as each of you, is in a very difficult situation now. Earth is experiencing a terrible strain connected with the impact of this so-called civilization of yours. Imagine how Earth and the elementals who maintain the order on Earth and look after the planet feel, bearing all the violence over nature that is committed in your world.

Only the influence of one loudspeaker, working at high volume, spreading the irregular beat of rock music, is enough for thousands of elementals to be shocked, and instead of fulfilling their duties connected with keeping order on the planet, they become ill or even die.

You should think not only about yourself. It is your duty to care about those inhabitants of planet Earth who evolve on the subtle plane. Think about the example that you show to your younger brothers, not to mention the fact that you should think deeply about the example that you show to your own children. None of your actions or words passes away without a trace.

Your actions, words, thoughts, and feelings exist in the subtle world as astral clichés. And in order to cleanse the planet from all of the human garbage accumulated on the subtle plane, an army of angels, elementals, and volunteers from other worlds is needed, as well as the best representatives of humankind who use their sleep during these long nights to participate in the cleaning of their native planet. In the morning they wake up exhausted, as if they didn't have that sleep at all. In fact, in their finer bodies those volunteers have been doing the hard work of cleansing the subtle planes of planet Earth from human garbage and have been giving help to ill elementals.

Today I have revealed to you the work being done by Beings of Light to cleanse your planet from the garbage of human thoughts and feelings. If this work was stopped even for a day, nothing would remain of planet Earth. It would cease to exist like many other planets that perished under the influence of non-divine civilizations.

Therefore, I come to you over and over again and urge you to come to your senses and to stop acting like those individuals who do not want to hear anything about God and about the Divine Law existing in this universe.

With the lapse of time everyone will receive what he has deserved. And Heaven's mercy is truly infinite.

I have visited you today to remind you of your responsibility to the evolutions of planet Earth and Life itself.

I AM Surya,
having been with you today.

The future of the planet and of millions of souls who are caught in the illusion and do not see that daylight depends on your ability to keep your consciousness pure, Heavenward, and in accordance with the Higher Worlds.

Lead by example! Be brave, be enduring, and be inventive. Invent the ways that will carry millions of people to a new level of consciousness. Do sound on the top note. Do set the pattern!

I am calling you into the future!

Archangel Michael
June 22, 2009

A **Message** to my disciples

Beloved El Morya,
December 23, 2007

A Message to my disciples

Beloved El Morya,
December 23, 2007

I AM El Morya, having come to you to give the next Message. The degree of importance of a particular Message for you, who are incarnated on Earth, is subjective. You cannot, being on your human level of consciousness, assess the significance of the phenomenon happening, nor its importance for further development of mankind.

Therefore, as a rule, we do not require you to make immediate and hasty decisions nor immediate action.

To be perfectly honest, the work that we carry out continuously with humanity of Earth could have much better results because the efforts exerted by us sometimes surpass all the allocated cosmic reserves. We clearly understand that it is very hard for you to look a little higher than the routine and bustle you have on a day-to-day basis. Therefore, we tirelessly come and give Messages that do not show much novelty, but they allow you to shake things up, and sometimes some phrase or expression in our Message makes you wake up so that you become able to carry out those actions in the physical plane that are necessary and that we constantly ask you to carry out.

So each time, with a lot of patience and persistence, I ask you to start acting, not just to read Dictations, prayers, Rosaries, or decrees. I ask you to implement real actions in the physical plane! Perhaps you do not quite understand what kind of actions I am talking about. I am neither asking you to overthrow the regime that exists in the state where you live nor to make a revolution or hold a mass meeting. I ask you to do ordinary human things that you mainly do anyway. But I ask you to do these things consciously. Consider each of your actions through the prism of the Moral Law, the Divine Law, existing in this Universe. I ask that every day you think about the consequences of your actions and reflect on every step you take.

Think about how you could ease your existence in the matter if every move of yours was in full accordance with the Divine Law existing in this Universe. You would not create new karma, and you could rapidly work off your past karma, making the right choices.

How easy it is! It is ingeniously simple! We come and constantly tell you about the same things. But why, why don't you hear us?!

Why do you read our Messages and five minutes later completely forget what you have read?! Why, even during the day, can't you stay under the influence of the right mental images that we send to you?

O God, it is sometimes unbearably difficult to work with embodied humanity! However, I am an optimist by nature, and I am sure that in a hundred of my Dictations or in a thousand of my Dictations, I will finally get a few hundred devoted disciples at my disposal that can sensitively listen to my guidance and follow my instructions. Believe me; I can see much better from my ascended state of consciousness what you should do and how you should behave.

The situation on Earth is moving in a better direction. It is not as sad as it was a few years ago, but we would like to get greater rates of your consciousness development. A reasonable solution was found, and thanks to that, the rate of your development will be accelerated. We will take care that the process of energy distribution becomes more even on the surface of Earth, so that Earth can survive and not become subjected to destructive cataclysm. We also learned how to localize clusters of negative energies that arise in human cities. If before such clots wandered the Earth's surface and brought unforeseen changes in remote locations, now all negative karma is localized at the source of its creation, and people in their experience can assess what "stinky" things they created themselves.

Thus, by means of your states you work off more quickly what you have generated.

And that is not all! We started thinking of establishing settlements on the globe that will be free from the influence of mass consciousness. Conditions for further development of human civilization can be created in such settlements. All who do not wish to develop must ultimately be isolated and eventually cut off like a dry branch that is found while doing garden work.

Everything that can grow and bear fruit should be transplanted into fresh fertile soil and blossom for the good of evolution of planet Earth.

Such are our plans, and I share these plans with you in the hope that there are people who approach me by writing personally and ask me to be in charge of their actions to transform the physical plane of planet Earth.

However, I have to calm you down immediately. I am a very strict and demanding Master. My students are able to produce many miracles in the physical plane, but I demand full and unconditional devotion, aspiration, and discipline from them in return. To those who are not confused by my high requirements, I say: "Welcome to my classes in the subtle plane, in my retreat, where I can meet you and guide your development."

As soon as I understand that you are quite ready to work with me, I will give you a task in the physical plane that you will have to implement. As a rule, many of my disciples are eliminated immediately as soon as they get a specific assignment from me.

They are more concerned about what they will get in return. When I explain to them that they have already received all that could be obtained, which is the opportunity to serve the Great White Brotherhood, this answer leads them into confusion, and they go off to wander in the illusion in search of more rewards, fame, money, and other things that are more valuable in their eyes.

I know that my Message will not be clear for many. However, my intention is not to be understood by millions, but rather, a few hundred faithful disciples are enough for me, and we will change the world in a few decades.

So, those who are not confused by my requirements, welcome and become my disciples.

I hear every sincere appeal to me that you say in your heart. If you do not hear a reply, it is only because you are very inattentive and too distracted by your illusion.

I have come to you today in order to give you reliable guidelines on your development.

I AM El Morya Khan.

Look around yourselves.

It is you and only you who are responsible for the imperfection of your world.

It is you and only you who may be blamed for all the hurricanes, natural calamities, tsunamis and extreme weather conditions.

These are the fruits of your hands and your consciousness.

Beloved Surya
May 10, 2005

A Teaching on how you should act in your lives

Lord Maitreya,
June 26, 2008

A Teaching on how you should act in your lives

Lord Maitreya,
June 26, 2008

I AM Maitreya, who has come to you in order to give you a short Teaching on how you should act in your lives. This Teaching I will give again through my Messenger.

So rare are the minutes of our communication. So rarely do we meet, except in a hurry when we find a minute to stay in silence.

I come to you when your thoughts become quiet, when your feelings calm down. I like to be in those places where even the wind goes down and one cannot hear the noise of the rain, when the whole of nature becomes quiet in anticipation of my arrival.

There will be a day on planet Earth when the entire planet waits with bated breath in anticipation of my arrival. That is the moment when I will come and I will be able to come into the incarnation. And you know that we and you are now preparing my forthcoming incarnation. For when the greater number of incarnated human individuals know me and follow my Teachings, the sooner that golden time will come when I will be able to be among people.

It has always been this way. First the grounds are prepared, and then a great incarnation comes into embodiment. And now we are starting our talk. I love so much to provide instruction to the hearts that are open to Love. I love so much to provide instruction in silence.

When you are able to attune to my vibrations in the silence of your heart, I will be able to associate with you, bypassing the Messenger. Yet, now we are procrastinating and waiting for you to be able to receive us in your hearts. That is because there are no conditions on Earth for us to come.

We expect that you will be able to listen to the Teaching that we are giving and create isles in your stormy ocean of life that are free from surges and storms — the isles where we will be able to give our Teaching in silence. You need to understand that the entire issue is in the difference of vibrations. When you change your vibrations, you become capable of hearing the subtle worlds and coming in contact with the Masters. We are different, yet we are similar. We are different because we reside in worlds with different vibrations, but we are similar, because you and I belong to the same evolutionary link of this universe. That is why I come to you.

Those who have had the chance to feel my vibrations understand that I want to come in contact and communicate with each of you very much. That is because when we meet, our worlds penetrate into each other, and we have the opportunity to merge in the stream of the Divine Love.

The spiritual world and the physical world are two sides of the same coin. When the moment comes, we will be able to attune to each other and talk to each other. In order to achieve that, you still have to work on yourselves a lot. I will tell you what qualities you are to acquire in order for our communication to happen.

First of all, you need to realize that there is a whole Hierarchy of cosmic beings. You are at the beginner levels of this Hierarchy. The honoring of the Hierarchy and its foundations is your primary duty. That is where such qualities as humility, discipline, and devotion evolve. Without these qualities you will be unable to advance on your Path. In order for you to acquire these qualities, you will need to part with the lion's share of your ego, which prevails in you at the current stage of your evolutionary development.

Your ego is the main obstacle to our communication with you. In order for you to step on the Path of Initiations, on which I teach you, you do not actually need to free yourselves from your ego completely, because without your ego, without your four lower bodies, you will not be able to reside in your world. All you need to do is to subject your ego to the Highest Law. You need to harness your beast of carnal desires and passions. We will train this beast conjointly.

Your understanding of our world will expand and your advancement on the Path will accelerate only when you become able to make constant efforts directed at multiplying Divine manifestations in your life and changing your entire lifestyle in accordance with the Divine models.

You cannot advance on your Path past a certain line until you get rid of the main imperfections and bad habits that accompany mankind at the current stage of its development. I am talking about alcohol, drugs, and nicotine consumption, listening to distortedly ragged rhythms of contemporary music, and the consumption of low-vibrational food, including meat.

Until you free yourselves from all these "pleasures" of your life, you will not be able to advance further on the Path of the evolution. That is because these intoxicating substances and energies entangle you like traps and you cannot go on.

I would not attract your attention to these issues if it were not essential for mankind to get rid of these imperfect manifestations right now. You talk a lot about your spiritual achievements, but how many of you can truly follow in your lives those behavioral and lifestyle models that correspond to our requirements, the requirements of the Ascended Hosts? You believe that you have achieved a lot and are able to understand and accept a lot in your consciousness, but I have to tell you that the majority of what you consume in the form of spiritual food, the spiritual teachings and practices of your times, are just the same substitutes as nicely packaged food substitutes that fill up the shelves of your grocery stores. You can and must establish order in your moral and spiritual guidelines. If you begin to persistently monitor and force out everything that is not Divine in your life, I guarantee you that favorable changes will come to Earth very soon. Everything is in your hands. You yourselves regulate the pace of your advancement on the path of the evolution and you even regulate the natural disasters that happen on your planet. That is because in the end, all natural disasters are caused by the negative energies that are produced by mankind.

Since we started giving Messages through our Messenger on a regular basis, we are following closely the general vibrational field of planet Earth. As you have been told before, there are areas on the planet where people read and accept our Messages with all their hearts; and there are entire areas that are closed from our energies. That is why there is an imbalance that is growing more and more. If you refer to the news headlines, you can easily determine that there are much more cataclysms and disasters in those regions and countries where people do not read our Messages and where there are no people who can transmit our energies and vibrations.

No matter how you want it, you will not be able to trick the Law. Sooner or later, mankind in general will accept our arguments and the Teaching that we give. We hope that it will happen as soon as possible.

**I AM Maitreya,
with Love to you.**

You hardly ever think about the impact that your thoughts and feelings have on everything that surrounds you.

In fact, all the negative effects that are present in nature, in weather conditions, in the financial sphere, and in any other spheres of life on planet Earth are generated by you yourselves. After some time, your own fruits materialize in the physical plane of planet Earth in the form of hurricanes, showers, droughts, or floods.

Beloved Kuthumi
July 2, 2009

About the situation in the world

Sanat Kumara
October 12, 2008

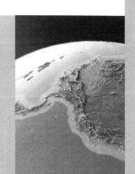

About the situation in the world

Sanat Kumara
October 12, 2008

I AM Sanat Kumara, having come to you today to give some explanations regarding the events taking place in the world. You know from the mass media reports that the financial situation in the world is unfavorable; you know about earthquakes that have become more frequent; you know about hurricanes and typhoons that almost constantly batter the shores of America and China. You also feel with your hearts much of what is not covered in the mass media but objectively exists in the subtle plane of planet Earth.

Yes, you are absolutely right. And indeed, all of this is just a slight and initial manifestation of the events that we warned you about. We have told you that changes are coming forth, and we have told you that the time has come and the vibrations of the physical plane of Earth are rising. Earth is moving up to a new energy level. Now the time has come when these vibrations have direct influence on the physical plane of planet Earth.

We have been so frank with you all this time, and we have warned you about the upcoming events. Why are you surprised?

We have given you recommendations for all occasions: how to behave, what to do, and what actions you are to undertake.

Do not say that everything is happening unexpectedly and that you did not know anything.

Reread our Messages that we have been giving through our Messenger. Read them carefully through the prism of what is happening in the world now. You will find not only the warnings but also concrete recommendations on how you should act, how you should behave, and how you should prepare for what is happening and what is about to happen.

You are in the physical plane, and you are troubled at the start by everything that is happening around you in the physical plane. Yet, we are calling you higher; we are calling you to Heavenly peaks, to our world. You will feel yourself in perfect security in our world, under safe control and care.

You are used to the fact that you come into your cozy physical world from embodiment to embodiment. You feel your unbreakable bond with your physical world. You have created this world. I am telling you that the time has come when you should understand and accept in your consciousness that your world will be transformed. For those individuals who have not reached a certain level of consciousness, the current incarnation may be the last manifestation of their individuality in the physical plane.

Think over my words while you still have some time. Accept with your hearts and try to manifest The Great Divine Law in your lives.

All things perishable that have been created by your imperfect consciousness will cease to exist. Only eternal things will remain: the best manifestations of your Spirit, unselfishness, sacrifice, devotion, the highest manifestation of Love, and many other things will exist with you in the New World. When the old world moves to non-existence, the New World will take its place.

There will be no place for any negative human manifestations in this world. Only that which is eternal and represents the manifestation of the best human qualities will remain in this world. And these qualities will multiply and grow. All the obsolete will be swept away and destroyed.

You have nothing to worry and grieve about. Trust the Great Law of the Universe. Nothing will happen to those who believe, to those who love, to those who have hope. Believe me.

I am with you. All the Ascended Hosts are with you. We will give our help all the way to everyone who still has the Divine Monad and in whom the Divine essence is manifested.

None of our people are to fall into non-existence. Everything will be as it is written in the Sacred Books of the past and present.

God is with you! Do not be afraid of the changes!

I AM Sanat Kumara. Om.

Do not be afraid of the changes in your lives or in the situation in the world.

Nothing can threaten you if you behave in a proper way and keep the Law properly.

None of the disasters or cataclysms can threaten those who faithfully serve God, who exists within all of Life and in each particle of Life.

Lord Maitreya
October 9, 2006

I am calling you into
the future!

Archangel Michael
June 22, 2009

I am calling you into the future!

Archangel Michael
June 22, 2009

I AM Archangel Michael.

I have come surrounded by the angels of the blue flame. Today, I would like you to fully concentrate your attention on the Message that I am giving you.

Now and for the coming days, the time has come when we must focus our efforts on helping the planet. And this is my Message and my warning to you.

I have been carefully choosing the words and thinking about how to convey to you the simple truth that you have reached the age when you have to share the responsibility for everything that happens on the planet, along with the Ascended Hosts.

You are not eager to take over this responsibility, yet you will have to take the responsibility for the planet. And this is the next level of consciousness to which you should rise.

You are still worried about what is happening around you, and you are so enthralled by the illusion that surrounds you at home, at work, and on television. However, there are much more important and substantial things, and the time has come for you to start thinking about these.

The entire world, the physical and the subtle planes of existence, are trembling because of many of your actions, thoughts, and feelings. Other beings of Light and I sometimes watch with a shudder as another burst of negative energy is released by humanity through its folly. Every time an uncontrolled release of negative energy happens, it takes great effort by numerous beings of Light to balance out the situation so that the consequences for the physical plane do not become catastrophic.

Now the time has come when you, the best representatives of the human community, must share with us, the Ascended Hosts, the responsibility for planet Earth and for everything that happens on the planet. And this is the level of consciousness that must be truly achieved by you in the nearest future.

Stop looking at the people that surround you; stop following the examples that you see around you and on television. For the time is coming when you should follow the direction that you get from your hearts. There are more subtle energies and processes that are occurring around you on the more subtle planes. And these processes are reflected within you as certain states of your consciousness. It is not always that the things occurring in the subtle planes can be consciously understood by you, and not everything reaches your external consciousness, but there is a certain intuition, premonition, or inspiration. And if you are honest with yourself, if you enter your heart and feel the vibrations of a more subtle plane, then you will undoubtedly hear the disturbing alarm that is ringing on planet Earth. And this alarm is a danger signal. It is an indicator of the trouble of the planet.

How can the situation be changed, and what can be done now in order for the preponderance of forces on the planet to open up an opportunity for a bright future again?

I think that it will not be superfluous to remind you that no matter how difficult the times are for you, and no matter how heavily the thoughts and states are filling you, you must find the strength to say:

"**I know that these states are not real. I know that the illusion is strong, but I am ready to oppose the illusory forces with all the power of my Love pouring from my heart. I love this world. I love God and His creation, and I will not allow this world to be destroyed. Beloved Archangel Michael and the angels of protection, I am asking you to use my lifestream to help the legions of Light. I know that nothing will happen to my planet as long as at least one light-bearer acts consciously on the side of the powers of Light.**"

As soon as we gather a sufficient number of individuals who are ready in their hearts to firmly support the Light, then we will be able to ask the Great Central Sun and all the Cosmic Council for mercy so that Earth gets help and this help comes without delay.

Much is at stake at this moment. Most human individuals are not ready for a change of consciousness. And volunteers are needed to demonstrate a new level of consciousness, the consciousness that is not tied to the physical or astral plane but is ready to cooperate with the Higher Worlds.

And when there are a sufficient number of individuals capable of demonstrating a new consciousness, then due to their efforts, the consciousness of other people will begin to change too.

You all are interconnected in more subtle planes of being. And there is a necessity for a higher frequency of consciousness to resonate like a tuning fork in space, so that the souls of those people who are stuck in the illusion rise again and cast their glances toward Heaven.

I envy those of you who are incarnated at this very difficult time, because the future of the planet and of millions of souls who are caught in the illusion and do not see the light depends on your ability to keep your consciousness pure, Heavenward and consonant with the Higher Worlds.

Lead by example! Be brave, be enduring, and be inventive. Invent the ways that will carry millions of people to a new level of consciousness. Do sound on the top note. Do set the pattern!

I am calling you into the future!

I AM Archangel Michael!

A Talk of vital importance

Beloved Kuthumi
July 2, 2009

A Talk of vital importance

Beloved Kuthumi
July 2, 2009

I AM Kuthumi. I have come to hold discourse.

I would like to talk to you openly, honestly, and directly.

My heart wishes to talk to you about many things but above all, of course, about something that is of the most interest and the most value for you at this stage.

The confusion that is present in your world is, of course, primarily caused by you yourselves. First, you perform irresponsible deeds and allow imperfect thoughts and feelings to seize hold of your being, and then you are astonished at the effects caused by your actions, thoughts, and feelings.

The mental field of the planet is overloaded with your negative states of consciousness. The same thing takes place on the astral plane.

You hardly ever think about the impact that your thoughts and feelings have on everything that surrounds you. In fact, all the negative effects that are present in nature, in weather conditions, in the financial sphere, and in any other spheres of life on planet Earth are generated by you yourselves. After some time, your own fruits materialize in the physical plane of planet Earth in the form of hurricanes, showers, droughts, or floods.

Many times we talked about the direct and immediate link that exists between your state of consciousness and everything that happens on planet Earth.

Your forgetfulness and constant hope that things will somehow become right by themselves make us, the Ascended Masters, doubt whether humanity is at all able to hear us and perceive the information that we give.

It has been said dozens of times that it is necessary to watch your thoughts and feelings, it is necessary to dedicate attention to the analysis of everything that happens to you during the day. It is just impossible to provide clearer signs on the physical plane. The next step is going to be a catastrophe of such magnitude that you can imagine but are afraid to even think about it.

Why do you read our Messages if you do not act according to our instructions and requests in your lives? It seems that humanity has come to the stage of its development when it is no longer able to adequately respond to the information.

In my Dictations, I have personally told you many times that you suffer from an excess of information. You overload your minds with various pieces of news and information that comes to you from different sources to such an extent that you have become not only incapable of discerning true information from false, but now you do not react to any information. You just let it pass by, and everything that flows into your consciousness during the day cannot stay there for a minute. The defense mechanism gets activated.

That is why I have come today to tell you one more time that you have to approach any information that you get very carefully. Even when it seems to you that the information passes by your consciousness, it has an ability to settle in your subconscious minds. And you can never tell when and what kind of influence your subconscious minds will exert on you, your choices, and your behavior.

The genie of permissiveness and accessibility of any information has been let out of the bottle. And the only way out of this situation is to protect yourselves against everything that is unnecessary for your evolutionary development. If you do not take steps in that direction, then the next generation will not be able to respond adequately to any information at all. Constant repetition influences your consciousness as coding. That is why you should expose yourselves to the influence of modern mass media with great caution. The time has come when you have to separate the wheat from the chaff in everything that surrounds you, and reject everything that is not Divine. I understand that when you are under constant pressure from all the modern, advanced technologies bombarding your consciousness at full power, 24 hours a day through hundreds of television and radio channels, it is hard for you to find your bearings and understand how to act in this situation.

We teach you discernment and the right choices that you can make. And the first and most reasonable thing is to limit the influence of all the mass media on your consciousness and subconsciousness. When that pressure lessens, you will gain an ability to navigate and to make the distinction. Your Higher Self, God within you, cannot talk to you; the Ascended Masters cannot talk to you while you are sealed off in the tons of informational trash that are poured out on you during the day from TV screens, radios, newspapers, and the Internet. You get a feeling that you are well-informed about all the latest events of the world, that you get information about all the innovations in all spheres. However, the most important news that is not broadcast on any of your radio or TV channels is not available for most of the people of Earth. The main news is the SOS signal that your planet and everything that lives on it is sending.

You are like a mad captain who navigates a ship in a storm. The collective consciousness and the collective subconscious of humanity are like this mad captain. And at any moment the ship — your planet — may strike sharp reefs and be shipwrecked.

You have tried; you have tasted all the fruits on planet Earth, and now the time has come when it is necessary to get back to more subtle manifestations of existence. How can you hear the sounds of music from my organ that I play every night in my retreat in the etheric octaves if you continuously deafen yourselves with all the background noise from your loud equipment?

Listening to silence, to the living voices of nature, is tiresome and boring for you. You have created an artificial civilization that has torn itself from everything that God created on planet Earth.

I have come in order to try one more time to deliver the simple truths to your consciousness. And I become silent in the hope that all of you have heard me.

I AM Kuthumi.

One imperfect thought or feeling attracts the same according to the vibration. And after a while, a hurricane of negative energy is formed that is manifested later in the physical plane in the form of real hurricanes and cataclysms.

Beloved Alpha
December 29, 2009

I **have come to warn** you that not everything is right on Earth

Elohim Hercules
December 26, 2009

I have come to warn you that not everything is right on Earth

Elohim Hercules
December 26, 2009

I AM Elohim Hercules. I AM a powerful Elohim of God. You may have heard some things about me in ancient myths and legends. But all the myths require keys in order to be deciphered and understood. The myths should not be repeated blindly. It is necessary to see what lies behind these myths. And it is not always that behind the myths are the events that took place on Earth. More often they describe the events that took place in the Higher planes of existence.

I AM serving on the ray of the Will of God. Power is my main quality — power and devotion to the Will of God. I am also responsible for the world of form so that the world of form continues its existence until the time that is specified, but only the Higher Masters and I know about it.

It may seem strange to you why I came to visit you today. I came to you today in order to warn you that not everything is right on Earth. Humankind continues rocking the boat with inconsiderate actions, thoughts, and feelings. There are especially many inconsiderate things at the end of the year when people celebrate the

New Year. I have to tell you that it takes only several days of such a celebration to create the same amount of karma that is created during the rest of the year. Therefore, before celebrating, think about which form is more suitable for you to do. Probably, it is better to change the traditional holiday concept of indispensable and uncontrollable drinking and gluttony.

If I had not kept the balance on the planet with all my might and power, the planet would have been broken into pieces long ago, like a walnut crushed under a huge rock. At present, the karma of humankind can destroy the planet in a fraction of a second.

It seems strange to you that I am so frank and talk about such terrible things. You think that I want to intimidate you or strike fear into you.

No, that's not something I am interested in. My only wish is to bring reason to the negligent children incarnated on planet Earth and to share with you the information about how much Divine Energy humankind owes to the cosmic bank. Every year at this difficult time of year, the Karmic Board receives Divine Energy as a credit on the Great Central Sun so that the evolutions of planet Earth can have a platform on which they will be able to evolve.

Each time we manage to convince the Higher Council of the Universe to provide energy. However, I know examples of other planets that when the moment came, the release of Divine energy for the maintenance of the physical platform was stopped. The planet was broken into pieces in a few seconds. The belt of asteroids between Mars and Jupiter is the memorial of the imprudent civilizations of a destroyed planet. Some of the representatives of this planet found shelter on Earth. And they, some of them, continue doing the same things, apparently believing in their immortality and impunity.

As an Elohim, I will do everything that I can for the maintenance and wholeness of the physical layer of planet Earth. However, I am unconditionally accountable to the High Council.

You, the humankind of Earth, continue your evolution thanks to the unlimited grace of Heavens. And if I were you, I would thank the Heavens 24 hours a day in all your temples for all the time remaining until the New Year.

If you prayed and meditated at least 10 percent of the time that you spend on entertainment, the Karmic Board would have arguments for the Central Sun.

However, this is not done. Do think about it.

Are there at least 10 righteous people among those who inhabit your cities? Are they capable of staying alone and having a prayer vigil for the benefit of the evolution of the Earth and for their salvation?

I come very rarely. And I am not wordy at all. It seems to me that I have already mentioned everything that is necessary.

I AM Hercules.

Each person is a generator of energies. It depends only on you to decide what kind of energies you send into the world.

Pallas Athena
December 28, 2011

You share the entire responsibility with the **Hierarchy** for what takes place on the planet

Beloved Alpha
December 29, 2009

You share the entire responsibility with the Hierarchy for what takes place on the planet

Beloved Alpha
December 29, 2009

... when you appear at the Karmic Board session in your finer bodies and you are given the last word, many of you, after watching the Akashic Records, are horrified by everything that you did, because you are shown not only your thoughts and states but also what has been caused by those imperfect states of your consciousness.

One imperfect thought or feeling attracts the same according to the vibration. And after a while, a hurricane of negative energy is formed that is manifested later in the physical plane in the form of real hurricanes and cataclysms.

At first, there was only one thought that caused a horrible cataclysm. Then, when you see this while you are facing the Karmic Board, you are horrified by the number of human lives that have been carried away because of you.

In order to become reasonable and to move to the next step of evolutionary development, humanity must be very careful in the manifestation of its thoughts and feelings because further evolution will be more dependent on your inner states.

Therefore, when you do not show any negative reactions but you have negative thoughts and feelings inside of you, it is just as destructive to the world as if you were throwing nuclear bombs.

With more refinement taking place on the planet, your thoughts and feelings gain larger influences — a much larger influence than your words and actions.

Prudence and caution are the qualities that you have to acquire. But you acquire these qualities automatically if devotion to the Will of God and a desire to serve your neighbor based on the feeling of unconditional Love are present inside of you.

Ignorance is the main quality you have to get rid of in the near future. It is incompatible with the next step of evolutionary development onto which humankind has to step due to the efforts of thousands of beings of Light who care about you.

I AM Alpha.
I have come in order to do my duty
for the humankind of Earth.

Peace on Earth
depends on the level
of consciousness
that the best sons
and daughters of
God are capable of
manifesting on Earth

Elohim Peace
January 4, 2010

Peace on Earth depends on the level of consciousness that the best sons and daughters of God are capable of manifesting on Earth

Elohim Peace
January 4, 2010

I AM Elohim Peace.

I have come to you with a desire to affirm peace in your world. I know that your world is still experiencing imperfect manifestations of consciousness such as wars and violence. I know that all this takes place in your world. That is why I have come to you on this day, at the beginning of the year.

I bring to you my hope and confidence that everything will change in your world. Wars are a temporary phenomenon in the history of humankind. Of course, you have studied history and can tell me that the entire history consists of wars, conquests, violence, and bloodshed.

I know this, beloved. But I also know that all of this is a temporary phenomenon, and a manifestation of your imperfect consciousness.

I also know that each of you living on Earth is a part of any bloodshed that takes place on Earth. At a certain level, you are all a single energy system. And where one person gives way to anger and aggression, a focal point of negative energy is created there that will be looking for a place on the globe where it can manifest itself.

You cannot say that only those who directly take part in a war are to blame for the wars and violence. No, it is simply a manifestation of the overall imperfection in the consciousness of humanity.

That is why I am calling on you to manifest peace in your hearts. When you become capable of controlling yourselves completely, when you are able to remain in a state of complete balance while everything around you is being destroyed, then the Ascended Hosts, and I personally will be able to pour the golden oil of peace on the planet. And we will extinguish the focus of any tension. All of this can be done beloved, and all of this is possible. All we need is a vessel on the physical plane, a person in embodiment who is capable of conducting the energies of peace into your dense world.

Yes, it seems like it should be very easy, but it is really very difficult to attain a level of consciousness in your world where you are able to conduct the absolute Divine consciousness of peace throughout all your life, or at least in some part of your life.

That is why wars and violence are still taking place in your world. I would like you to start thinking today about what you personally can do for the sake of peace.

Once again, I repeat that there is something present in each of you that allows aggression to remain in the world. You will not be able to instantly attain this new state of consciousness, free from aggression and the desire to punish. In fact, the roots of this consciousness go back centuries to a time when people had already lost the Divine models in their consciousness. It began to seem to them that God was too slow to punish those, who in their opinion needed to be punished.

The illusion became so dense that people lost the Divine vision and the Divine guidelines. They decided to replace Divine justice with their own actions.

In their opinion, evil had to be punished, and if they didn't do it, who would?

The karma of the first murder in the name of God, in the name of justice and goodness, has become so entangled over these countless millennia that it is impossible to stop the descent of such karma in an instant. Any karma, being energy, must exhaust itself.

Therefore, it is impossible to stop all the violence throughout the entire world starting tomorrow. It can be dreamt of, it can be aspired to, but the karma of violence must exhaust itself.

Yet, you know that the return of karma can happen in different ways. The karma of violence can return to you in the form of a third world war. But this can be prevented, if a sufficient number of individuals firmly decide not to commit violence in their lives, and turn the other cheek every time they get slapped; if a sufficient number of individuals are able to manifest such a level of consciousness, then the karma of violence and wars will be extinguished by the manifestation of the qualities of peace in the hearts of these people.

I am talking about the level of consciousness of Christ and Buddha. Only at this level of consciousness is it possible to acquire the qualities of inner peace and calmness to the fullest.

That is why I am calling you to perfect your consciousness in order to serve the world like Jesus served during his incarnation 2000 years ago.

The world needs your service. Peace on Earth depends on the level of consciousness that the best sons and daughters of God are capable of manifesting on Earth. Now your time has come, when you must do this. There is no way to postpone it any longer.

I came to you today with the good news about peace on Earth. And this peace fully depends on you, on your inner peace that you must attain by your own effort.

I AM Elohim Peace.

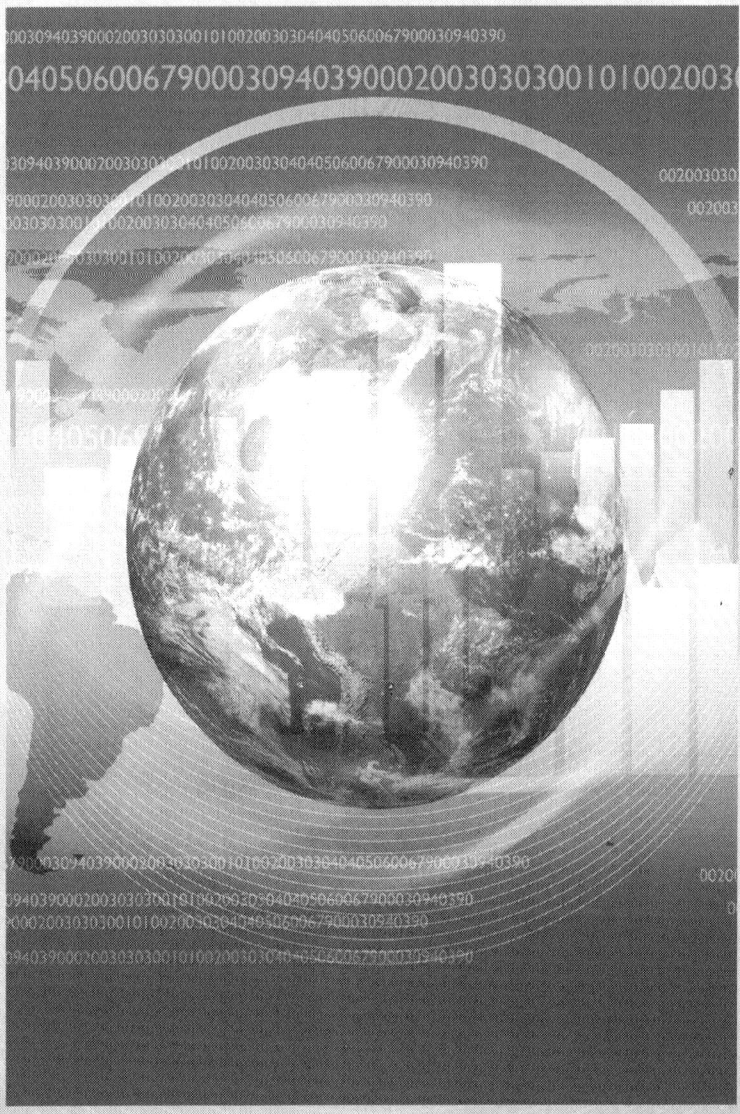

A Teaching about the situation on the planet

Master Hilarion
January 18, 2010

A Teaching about the situation on the planet

Master Hilarion
January 18, 2010

I AM Hilarion.

I have come to you again on the ray of Truth, science, and healing.

Today, I would like to use this Divine opportunity for the transmission of the Messages into your world, in order to give the Teaching about how you should attune yourselves to current events.

The moment, the turning point, after which everything will start to change in your world has come. Those of you who have devotion to the Great White Brotherhood in their hearts are tired of waiting for the times when the changes that the Masters keep on describing in their Messages, will begin taking place on Earth.

Beloved, everything is changing already. And your level of consciousness simply does not let you understand the full scale of the changes that are happening on Earth. A faster pace of changes is just physically impossible because we have to maintain the balance on the planet and simultaneously purify the planet from everything old and obsolete. Our service to the evolutions of planet Earth at times resembles walking along the edge of a knife. We must strictly maintain balance so as not to fall to the right or to the left.

On the one hand, the vibrations of the planet are rising. It is obvious. Even secular science captures the changes that occur in the base frequency of Earth and its magnetic field. These new conditions are tolerated very poorly by the individuals who have chosen to serve the forces that are opposite to us. They feel ill at ease. And in order to get back to their normal state, they have to strengthen the effect of the tested methods that have always caused the lowering of vibrations: alcohol, nicotine, sex, low-frequency music, gambling, drugs, and aggression. This list can be continued.

My mission is to bring to your consciousness an understanding of the ongoing events. So, on the one hand, a great number of people tolerate the elevation of the vibrational level of the planet very poorly because their level of consciousness is not ready for the changes. On the other hand, those people who are ready for the changes and who naturally have high vibrations and high sensitivity, also lose their bearings while living amidst all this hell, as they perceive what they are surrounded by in this world as hell. They could be living very successfully in the current vibrational field of this planet. However, at the same time, this planet is also inhabited by individuals for whom the rising vibrations are life threatening, and they try to use everything in order to extend their existence as much as they can and protect their lifestyles without changing anything in them. Such coexistence of two individuals with completely different inner natures simultaneously in one city, in one house, causes bewilderment and lack of understanding on the part of the light-bearers.

I have come today once again, to provide an understanding of the processes taking place on Earth. And now you understand the difficulty of our mission. If there is only one or several light-bearers among a million people in a city, while the rest of the city's population has chosen the carnal world, then we have to hold back nature's forces, so that this city does not get destroyed in order to save just this one soul or several souls.

You will not understand some of the principles by which we are guided. However, we act strictly in accordance with the Cosmic Law, and believe me, all of the resources for saving souls are used at 1000 percent capacity. Sometimes it is necessary to change the natural processes taking place on planet Earth just to save one soul.

You have probably read in our Messages that a decision has been made to further increase the vibrations of the planet.

And you are probably following the news reports about the increase in seismic activity on the planet.

These processes can be explained. When the vibrations of the planet are rising, but people's consciousness restrains the increase of the vibrations, then centers of tension are formed in the subtle field of Earth, which are manifested on the physical plane in the form of seismic activity, hurricanes, and man-made disasters.

Do understand that we are not the cause of all these troubles. All these calamities are caused solely by the negative energies generated by humanity.

If you imagine for a moment that at least 10 percent of human individuals living on the planet followed the path shown by us, the whole situation on the planet would go along a smoother path. In fact, the work of the Ascended Hosts is focused, as much as possible, on alleviating the attacks that humanity on Earth will have to face. This is where we spend the vast majority of the energy provided to us by the Great Central Sun.

Now I would like to touch upon one more topic.

I would like to give a helping hand to those individuals who have chosen the Light, but because of their karma, for the time being, they cannot escape the life circumstances that surround them. I understand very well how difficult it can be for you. However, first the karmic energy must completely exhaust itself, and you will have to resign yourselves to accept it. Secondly, God always gives you the opportunity to go along an easier path; however, because you are burdened with a great karmic load, you do not always see that path. Therefore, ask the Masters for help more often. Address the Master with whom you feel the closest connection. You can express your requests in writing or ask to travel to our retreats before you go to sleep, so that by the next morning, your outer consciousness can receive the information on how to find the way out of the enclosure of karma that surrounds you. Do not hesitate to ask that you be shown the way out of your karmic situation. One thing should be noted: write down your requests; inscribe them on paper. And then several years later, when you read what you had asked for, you will discover with surprise that all your requests have been granted. And this will be the best proof for you that the Great White Brotherhood exists and never leaves its comrades without protection and help.

I tried to bring home to you this information, that perhaps will support you and will serve as a helping hand from your elder brother.

I AM Hilarion.

Meditate on Good, Weal, and Love.

Keep internal peace and quietness.

Each of you should become a fulcrum on Earth, a conductor of Light. This Light will help you equalize the balance of your planet. This Light will help Earth in ascending to the next level of evolution.

Sanat Kumara
March 22, 2005

A Teaching on responsibility

Sanat Kumara,
June 1, 2010

A Teaching on responsibility

Sanat Kumara,
June 1, 2010

I AM Sanat Kumara, coming to you through our Messenger again.

I have come today to remind you of the current situation on the planet again and of your responsibility for the situation on Earth. When humankind is able to realize the whole fullness of responsibility for everything that happens on Earth, we will be able to breathe with relief. So long as humankind has the consciousness level of a child, we are forced to take care of it and watch that the children of Earth, because of their thoughtlessness, do not make such a mess that life on the planet becomes impossible.

Now that I have alerted you a little to my understanding of the situation on the planet, I am ready to give a small Teaching that will be useful for you to listen to.

Because your consciousness cannot concentrate on something specific for a long time, we have to come many times to remind you of very simple truths that you probably know but for some reason have forgotten to put into practice and hold in your consciousness.

I have come after a long break in our work with humankind of Earth through this Messenger. And all that time I had an opportunity to watch the development of events on the planet from the subtle plane. You also had an opportunity to watch the development of events but only from your physical plane. And those people who are thoughtful and analytical could notice that the situation on the planet becomes more strained every day. And practically ceaseless earthquakes, volcanic eruptions, military conflicts, acts of terrorism, social explosions, and coups that happen here and there on the globe give clues about the situation on the planet.

It seems to you that it is natural and there is nothing unusual in it. Indeed, all those features of undeveloped human consciousness have existed before. They have existed for several hundred years. But the frequency and the scale of those negative phenomena and those negative forces that stand behind those phenomena have never been so large.

Let me tell you that my memory is much better than the memory of currently incarnated humans of Earth. And I have an opportunity to look into the Akashic Records and compare your situation with any of the situations that have ever existed on Earth. The result of that comparison won't be in favor of the current situation. We, the Ascended Hosts need more and more energy to hold the situation on the planet and to prevent the most horrible occurrence for humankind in which the physical platform itself would become destroyed.

It seems to you that I speak about something that has no immediate reference to you, as if somebody's actions somewhere else led to the imbalance on Earth that manifested in volcanic eruptions and tornadoes. Beloved, do not think so categorically. All currently incarnated individuals on Earth are so closely interwoven with their karma that it is impossible to distinguish who and what action led to a catastrophe that is going on now on Earth.

The informational field of humankind relates more and more to the general informational field in which it is impossible to pick out the contribution of a separate individual. The development of modern mass media led to the fact that the news reaches the most distant places on the globe in a fraction of a second. And every man that resonates on the news makes his contribution to the energy situation on Earth.

Not all of the news draws a wide response. And most information is hidden from humankind because if humankind knew all the information about the destructive impacts of all that is happening on the planet now, the resonance in the minds of people would have an uncontrolled character.

Your weak memory and inability to realize the whole burden of the current situation on the planet is actually quite fortunate for you.

It requires a very lofty consciousness to hold the entire existing imbalance on the planet and balance it with its own inner achievements. I will let you in on a secret that there are a definite number of incarnated individuals who undertake the task of balancing the energies on the planet. And it is thanks to those selfless souls that Earth has an opportunity to exist.

However, those of you who are reading these lines now need to devote more time to the inner work on yourselves, for only because of your inner achievements is it possible to balance the situation at every point of the planet where you live.

There are certain people who are continuing to rock the boat by virtue of their own ignorance. But those people waste the last crumbs of their good karma, littering the informational field of the planet even more.

Every low-grade thought of yours is multiplied millions of times. You can watch the analog of that process on the Internet. There are a lot of places in that virtual space where a man, often under a fictitious name, says ridiculous things, deliberately lies, or talks nonsense. And you can see how quickly thousands of simpletons flock together on that "news" and spread it all over the Internet.

That is how you create karma, not noticing it and without being aware of your actions. One of the basic and cornerstone Teachings that was given by us through our Messenger is the Teaching on the careful attitude toward spending the Divine Energy. You are responsible for every erg of the Divine Energy that you receive from the Divine World. And the way that you consume the Divine Energy weaves either an immortal body of Light for you or a web that ties you to the physical plane of Earth forever and closes your opportunity for further growth in the subtle and loftier worlds.

Today I have given the Teaching that reminds you of your responsibility. I think that in the current situation on the planet, it won't do any harm to listen to that Teaching once again.

I AM Sanat Kumara. Om

Everyone is given a chance to survive. Everyone is given a helping hand. But the Law of free will does not allow intervention if there is no call for help from your side.

Yet even when the situation is completely hopeless because of the karma you have created, even when the utmost sinner is beseeching Heaven's help at the eleventh hour, we have no right to refuse help.

So, call for help, and help will come! Pray for salvation, and salvation will come! Trust in God, and God will protect and guide you!

Beloved Babaji
June 25, 2011

A traditional **Message** at the beginning of the year

Gautama Buddha
January 1, 2011

A traditional Message at the beginning of the year

Gautama Buddha
January 1, 2011

I AM Gautama Buddha.

I have come today to once again talk about vital things, to speak about what is happening on planet Earth and what is still ahead for the planet.

We have said many times that the vibrations of the planet are rising. The rise of vibrations is a necessary process. And this process was planned by the supreme management body of this Universe.

Unfortunately, this seemingly good event connected with the rise of vibrations is not a very comfortable and joyful event for the common, ordinary human individuals who are incarnated today.

The rise of the vibrational frequency impacts on all of your bodies.

Your physical body and your more subtle bodies get into a field of vibrations unusual for them. When you are in your own vibrations, inherent in you, you feel comfortable. Once you get to an uncharacteristic

154

level, you start feeling discomfort. This can manifest as diseases of your physical body or various inferior mental states, such as a feeling of fear, aggression, depression, or unwillingness to live.

Inferior states of consciousness can lead to mass unrest and man-made disasters of various degrees. That is because your technocratic civilization relies too heavily on different kinds of equipment that require high-quality performance from the workers who serve it. Therefore, now the whole planet, especially those regions where there is a highly developed civilization, is entering a high-risk zone.

Inferior states of human consciousness lead not only to man-made disasters but also to natural disasters. You know that during the last one hundred years, the number of various natural disasters, such as volcanic eruptions, earthquakes, and tsunamis, has increased several times. And this is a consequence of the tension on the astral plane caused by your state of consciousness.

Therefore, we come time after time and give our recommendations and warn about the technical safety rules that are necessary to follow so that life on Earth can continue.

We ask you to restrict the influence of mass consciousness on yourself and your children. This concerns the restriction of watching television programs, listening to radio programs, and listening to low-quality music. We also ask you to limit the use of meat, not to consume alcohol, drugs, and nicotine, and not to play aggressive computer games.

These are very simple requirements. And I will explain why it is necessary to fulfill these requirements. All of the things I have listed above bring about a fall in your vibrations. And consequently, you are forced to be in discord with the general vibrational background of Earth, which rises year after year. So, if you were allowed to do all those things in former times, now they become dangerous for you. And they become more and more dangerous from year to year.

Many people try to lapse into a state of comfort by increasing their doses of alcohol or nicotine and listening to the new kinds of so-called "music"; however, this makes you go deeper and deeper into negative states of consciousness.

We offer you simple recipes. We suggest that you use all the means available to you to maintain your consciousness at the highest possible level. In this case, your vibrations are in phase with the vibrational background of the planet, and you are able to remain on the evolutionary path of development.

Unfortunately, big cities, being the centers of mass consciousness, are unable to withstand the pace at which the vibrational level of the planet is rising. Life in big cities will become very dangerous over the course of time. In our Messages we have also told you about the necessity of living in harmony with nature.

A few more years will pass, and you will search for these Dictations of ours as if for your grandmother's recipe for New Year's pie, and try to follow what we ask of you.

However, just as the products that your grandmother used to make that pie with the taste that you remember from your childhood are no longer available, these recipes of ours can already be useless in a few years.

Just like the products in the shops have the same names like they used to have, but they are not the same now because they contain artificial surrogates, so too is the spiritual food offered to you by your mass media just a surrogate that you habitually devour without feeling any satisfaction.

The existing civilization has reached a deadlock. And the only way out of this impasse is to raise your head and aspire upward to God. You have to make your choice consciously and decide what the priorities in your life are: you with all your carnal desires or God.

You should try to give your answer to this question before the end of this year.

We give our Messages with the hope that at least a few hundred or even just tens of people will be able to awaken from the illusion of the surrounding world and stir up the rest.

The battle is raging for every soul. Each of you who read our Messages is dear to us. We are ready to do much for you, but you should take the first step and ask us for help.

Only when you realize that you are following the wrong path and ask us for help will we send a guide who will lead you to the Path of Light.

As long as you doubt and think that we are simply telling you scary stories, we cannot provide you with the help that you really need.

I have come with a traditional Message at the beginning of the year, and I have given you all the necessary recommendations.

I AM Gautama Buddha.

It is only your desire to change that is required. It is your wish to serve the evolutions of planet Earth that is required. Do not miss the opportunity that is opening up now!

It is hard to comprehend when all is well. The realization comes much more quickly when the situation grows so absurd that even the deaf and the blind start to realize that something is going wrong.

That is why I do not get tired of coming and keep shouting in your ears, "The time has come!" The time has come to make a revolution in your consciousness!

Beloved Babaji
June 25, 2011

By unfettering
yourselves from
low states of
consciousness,
**you save the whole
world**

Beloved Quan Yin
June 24, 2011

By unfettering yourselves from low states of consciousness, you save the whole world

**Beloved Quan Yin
June 24, 2011**

I AM Quan Yin. I have come today with an unusual Message. This Message is being dictated by time and necessity.

...

Cataclysms, manifestation of aggression in the form of acts of terrorism, wars, and revolutions all of these are the consequences of an unbalanced state of consciousness of the people on Earth. You know this, and you have heard this Teaching many times on how to avoid cataclysms on the planet.

There is a direct and permanent connection between the state of consciousness of people and various disasters that occur on the planet. When people's consciousness deteriorates, cataclysms increase. This is a part of the process of interconnection of all living things. Therefore, the task of the Ascended Masters and my task as the goddess of Mercy and Compassion are to minimize those inevitable consequences that are caused by the imperfect consciousness of people.

As you can see from the statistics, the number of catastrophes, volcanic eruptions, earthquakes, man-made disasters, and severe weather conditions are increasing year after year. And since those cataclysms that are taking place at this time were formed by the level of consciousness that humanity had several years ago and even several decades ago, it is not difficult to predict the future growth of cataclysms, disasters, misfortunes, diseases, and other troubles.

The only way out of this unfavorable situation and impasse is a rapid change in the consciousness of the incarnated humanity, a rapid positive and qualitative leap of consciousness where the bulk of humankind rises to a new level of consciousness.

It is a desirable and quite achievable goal. And if we bear in mind the law of cyclical development of humankind, it means that if the pendulum has swung in one direction, then sooner or later it will swing in the other direction. Our task is to minimize the possible consequences of excessive deviation from the evolutionary path of human development.

The whole arsenal of means that the Ascended Masters wield is now set into motion. And if you could add your efforts to ours, then together we could cope much more quickly and more successfully with the consequences of humanity's wrong choices.

A more balanced and successful development and your entry into the period of the Golden Age are created by the vectors of the consciousness of positively directed individuals. The more human individuals there are who are able to balance themselves, the surrounding people and conditions, and the greater efforts and aspirations they demonstrate, the sooner humankind will enter the passage of sustainable and stable development.

This simple thought is communicated in various ways to those individuals who can perceive our Teaching, and with the help of these Messages as well. There is always hope for you to enter the passage of steady development, but there is also a possibility that the situation will get out of control. So, there is very little time left for your consideration.

All that you can really do is to change your approach to everything around you. There are deviations from the Divine Path of development in all spheres of human activity.

The system of education not so much educates the future generations as much as it deprives them of their wish to learn and to self-perfect in God.

The public health service takes away the rest of people's health.

The financial system is not tied to the results of creative labor but to the mental and emotional swings of the people who gamble on the stock exchange and manage funds.

The political system is completely detached from people's needs, and serving the weak and poor members of society is replaced by serving the personal interests of separate individuals.

Mass media spreads anything except information (rumors, gossip, scandals, and criminal stories).

All spheres of human activity should be transformed in accordance with the Divine Law; otherwise, they will not be able to exist.

Mankind has arrived at such a point in its development where non-existence is already clearly evident. We make one attempt after another to change the situation. And it is through Divine Mercy that we continue giving our directions through the transmission of our Messages. We throw a life buoy to those who are still capable of emerging from the waters of illusion, seizing this practically last chance that the Heavens are giving.

At the existing level of human consciousness, only a few are able to evolve without the physical platform. The rest of the people need a physical platform to continue evolution. So we count on those few people who we are trying to help.

Even if only a few people manage to achieve a new level of consciousness as a result of reading our Messages, we will insist on the opportunity to give our Messages, and we will come with our talks and directions again and again.

In conclusion of my Message today, I would like you to realize the full responsibility for the situation on the planet. If you could obtain my level of consciousness just for several seconds and see your actions with my eyes, I think that your consciousness would change very quickly.

You resemble the people who continue their party while planet Earth is trying to save its physical platform from destruction with all its remaining might.

The feast of life is over. The time has come for hard inner work. By unfettering yourselves from low states of consciousness, you save the whole world. This is because everything is interconnected in our worlds. And a beat of a butterfly's wing is heard as thunder in the subtle worlds. What, then, is the effect of your actions, thoughts, and feelings?

I AM Quan Yin.

Then, when your vibrations are in harmony with the changes that are taking place, you feel enthusiasm, joy, and love. You are happy and purposeful.

When your vibrations come into conflict with the new energies, you feel dissatisfaction, fear, and aggression.

The key to changing your state of consciousness will be your desire to follow the Creator's Plan... Welcome the new energies, the energies of regeneration, and follow them!

Pallas Athena,
December 28, 2011

The time has come to make a revolution in your consciousness!

Beloved Babaji
June 25, 2011

The time has come to make a revolution in your consciousness!

Beloved Babaji
June 25, 2011

I AM Babaji.

I have come for a decisive talk today. And my determination must be passed on to those of you who are consonant with my vibration of transformation.

When I was incarnated, I kept saying that a revolution is on the way. And all the deadlines established for the beginning of the revolution have already lapsed. Therefore, get ready for the changes that will be truly revolutionary! And these changes must take place within your consciousness. And as soon as they happen in your consciousness, everything around you will instantly start burning in the fire of revolution, because everything that is now running the show will be swept away — your entire familiar ambience, everything you are used to, all your habits and attachments.

It will inevitably happen because none of this complies with the Divine plan or meets the conditions of the evolutionary path of human development.

When persuasion does not work, and people are obstinate and do not obey the law, then force is used. When humankind does not obey the Divine Law, and the terms allowed for coming to awareness are expiring, it is necessary to apply enforcement methods of influence.

The things that you are used to and perceive as integral parts of your existence, in fact and for the most part, do not correspond to what should exist at this stage of evolutionary development. Therefore, many spheres of human activity are to undergo truly revolutionary changes.

You are used to eating meat and meat products. You will have to give them up because the vibrations of the physical plane are rising, and in order for your physical body to be in harmony with these vibrations, you should switch to some higher vibrational types of vegetable food.

You are used to drinking alcohol. You will have to give it up immediately, once and for all. The same goes for tobacco and drugs.

You have a habit of using your sexual energy without limitation. You will have to become chaste because the vitality of the future generation of people will depend on the extent to which you will be able to preserve your sexual potential. All the unviable will not be able to exist in the new world.

You are used to getting pleasure from watching TV. You will have to break this habit because you will need the quality of concentration on the Higher reality, and everything that fills your TV and radio airwaves prevent you from concentrating on the Higher reality.

You see that the changes to come will wipe away at least half of your industries and businesses, the entire mass entertainment industry, and the production of drugs and low-quality food products.

These are truly revolutionary changes. And all this must happen. Only in this case will humankind be able to manifest its capability for further evolutionary growth.

On one side of the scale, there are all those "blessings" of your civilization that I have mentioned above, to which humanity is attached and still does not want to part with for the time being. On the other side of the scale is the very existence of planet Earth, the physical plane of planet Earth.

You have to decide on a tight historical time frame. The more time your contemplation takes, the less likely a seamless transition will be made and the greater the probability that a global cataclysm will destroy an unsuccessful civilization.

All this is because of your reluctance to change and your unwillingness to follow the Divine Law.

The Divine Law assumes that society should be based on completely different principles: when a person is able to increasingly manifest his Divine nature. Your civilization contributes to a person manifesting his devilish nature. Thus, the issue of choice is timely. And the choice mostly concerns whether you desire to follow the path of evolutionary development or to join the garbage dumps of unsuccessful civilizations of the past.

The Path is open for those of you who make the right Divine choice within yourselves and follow this choice, despite the fact that all those around you keep on following their old ways, detached from God and the Divine guidance. Even if something happens to the planet, you will get a pass to other worlds that are consonant with your vibrations.

Therefore, we count every person who can prove his right to ascend to the next evolutionary stage.

You have been told about a vast opportunity that is opening up. You have been told that it is easy for you to change now, because the entire Heaven gives you help and support. And it is truly a blessed time in which you live. Some individuals are evolving at a rapid pace. Others are just as rapidly sliding down.

Everyone is given a chance to survive.

Everyone is given a helping hand.

But the Law of free will does not allow intervention if there is no call for help from your side.

Yet even when the situation is completely hopeless because of the karma you have created, even when the utmost sinner is beseeching Heaven's help at the last possible moment, we have no right to refuse help.

So, call for help, and help will come!

Pray for salvation, and salvation will come!

Trust in God, and God will protect and guide you!

It is only your desire to change that is required.

It is your wish to serve the evolutions of planet Earth that is required.

Do not miss the opportunity that is opening up now!

It is hard to comprehend when all is well. Awareness comes much faster when the situation grows so absurd that even the deaf and the blind start to realize that something is going wrong.

That is why I do not get tired of coming and keep shouting in your ears, "The time has come!"

The time has come to make a revolution in your consciousness!

I AM Babaji.

The more humanity will defend the old way of life and the former stereotypes of behavior supported by mass consciousness and by the negative impact of the majority of the media, including the Internet, the more severe tests humankind may undergo in the near future.

Conversely, if qualitative changes take place in the consciousness of people, such as a leap of consciousness toward the Divinity, then the more smoothly the changes will take place.

Quan Yin
December 29, 2011

Welcome the
new energies,
the energies of
regeneration, **and
follow them!**

Pallas Athena,
December 28, 2011

Welcome the new energies, the energies of regeneration, and follow them!

**Pallas Athena,
December 28, 2011**

I AM Pallas Athena and I have come to you in order to give my Message. I seldom come; however, today it is my turn to address you, those who hear me and heed my words.

Many hundreds and even thousands of years ago I was known and revered on Earth. Now only a few people know my name. Nevertheless, my words will be significant for many people because the time has come. The time has come for the knowledge of the Truth, and its interpretation within your consciousness will bring humanity closer to an important stage, which humankind is now standing on the threshold.

It is difficult for you to imagine the opportunity that is opening up before humankind. However, a short historical period of time will pass and everything will change because your consciousness will change, beloved. It is already changing. The reason for the changing of your consciousness is the cosmic timeframe that has approached. And these terms are paving the way for your transition to a new energy level.

Just like when the people of the plains get into the mountains and they feel discomfort and malaise, now you also feel a bit out of place. The time has changed, and the vibrations of the planet have changed. It is as if you have been moved in space to a different, more elevated place. Although it seems to you that the same reality remains around you, everything is changing and has already changed. That is why within your consciousness grand changes are taking place now. Every step requires great effort because the space has changed.

When you come up to an apple tree and start shaking it, the ripe apples fall from the branches and so do the worm-eaten ones and the withered, never-ripened fruits. That is exactly what is happening to humankind. The vibrations have raised, and just like shaking an apple tree, it makes you leave your old haunts and move.

Changes are coming to all spheres of life and society. It is not because someone gave the command but due to the fact that the time has come, and there is no other way. Each change will correspond to the Creator's Plan for the next stage of evolutionary development. And even if you resist with all your being and defend old approaches, old stereotypes of behavior, and old habits, you will still have to yield to the Divine Plan.

You are observing this process all around you when, due to the raising of vibrations, all your inner problems have been aggravated. Hence, so have the problems of the society you live in and the problems of the whole human community. This applies to all spheres of human life.

A new stage has arrived, and the sooner the consciousness of society can comprehend and adjust to the new conditions, the fewer will be the number of losses, social explosions, and cataclysms you will encounter in the near future. The key that will help you act in the new environment will be the comprehension that the coming age will be associated with the transition to the level of more Divine relationships between people. You will feel the necessity to restore morality in society. You will feel the attraction of relationships based on friendship, cooperation, mutual help, and love.

Everything that is now on the sidelines of your interests will return to your life again. And it will not be the ostentatious positive qualities that you at times demonstrate in communicating with each other. It will be the genuine Divine qualities that grow from your hearts and gradually embrace the whole world.

The return of humankind to eternal values will take place. Everything that is old, everything that is segregating, everything that is based on fear and separation from God will gradually be replaced by the new qualities, Divine qualities, and eternal qualities.

People are tired of hypocrisy and rudeness. The coming age will revive the fine arts. The new generation will aspire to manifest the patterns of the Divine world in the physical plane. And no matter how the past will resist, its time is up. The new consciousness, new relationships, and the new world are coming!

Now the most difficult stage is taking place: the stage of transition to the new consciousness and new way of thinking. That is why your time is special and interesting.

I appeal to the souls of those people who remember me. There was a time when you used to come to the temples dedicated to me, and I was able to communicate directly with your souls. Now you have to recollect your mission. Your hearts carry within them the Truth that must be manifested in the physical plane. You are the people for whom the time has come to act.

The changes around you will obediently reflect the changes coming from your hearts. Each person is a generator of energies. It depends only on you to decide what kind of energies you send into the world.

Then, when your vibrations are in harmony with the changes that are taking place, you feel enthusiasm, joy, and love. You are happy and purposeful.

When your vibrations come into conflict with the new energies, you feel dissatisfaction, fear, and aggression. The key to changing your state of consciousness will be your desire to follow the Creator's Plan. Believe me, for you there is no point in resisting. Welcome the new energies, the energies of regeneration, and follow them!

You need to accept the new energies. You need to control every movement of your thoughts and cut off from yourself everything that does not lead you along the path of your ascension to the Truth.

**I AM Pallas Athena,
and I have been with you today.**

All changes will
come to your world
from within you

Quan Yin
December 29, 2011

All changes will come to your world from within you

Quan Yin
December 29, 2011

I AM Quan Yin. I have come.

Today we will talk again about eternal topics, about the everlasting. Because there is so much fuss in your world, it is extremely rare to find something that belongs to eternity.

The most important thing that you lack in your lives is the sense of the Divine, Eternal Law that is present in the universe and permeates the entire universe. Then, when you are able to raise your consciousness to the Divine, you detach from the illusion and are able to perceive that which is everlasting.

There are qualities that are eternal and present within each of you. And you should seek these Divine qualities in the depths of your hearts and spread them to the world around you.

You are waiting for changes in the reality around you. You anticipate the coming changes and expect them. Now the time has come for you to understand that all of the changes that are coming will come to your world from within you. For that you should approach the Divine reality in your consciousness.

When you are able to move within yourselves and enter the secret abode of your heart, then you can bring the transformations closer to your world.

This is the Path that we never tire of repeating to you: the Path that lies within your hearts.

Believe me, there are not any changes outside of you that will bring the Golden Age of humanity closer. These changes will come from inside of your being.

Everything that now exists in the external world distracts you from the Truth lying in your hearts. Retreat into the silence of your hearts, and feel the peace and the bliss of eternity. From that point you can have the right view on everything that surrounds you in the external world.

Since I have come at the end of the annual cycle, it is my duty to give you an idea about the forthcoming transformation. You see that the energies of regeneration are beginning to penetrate more and more actively into your world and into your consciousness. And the question is to what extent you will manage to overcome your external consciousness and give preference to the inner transformation. Now, at the least, my words seem strange for many people because I am speaking about the changes that are not visible from a merely human view. I am speaking about the subtle processes that take place inside of your being. And these subtle processes exert much more influence and effect on your world than any external actions. Any manifestations in the external world — cataclysms, natural calamities, rallies and revolutions, wars, and terrorist acts — are secondary.

And it is possible to avoid all of this easily if only you exerted yourself and carefully read our Messages and listened to the advice that we are giving to you.

Any of the most subtle impulses of your soul cause inevitable changes in the physical world. If you experience the states of happiness, love, and peace, you exert an influence on vast distances around you — and perhaps even on the whole planet. The more subtle, Divine feelings you experience, the more influence you have on the surrounding physical world. That explains why a small number of saints can balance the situation on the whole planet.

Negative feelings and thoughts also have an influence on the physical world. Fortunately, because they have low vibrations, these energies do not have significant influence, since they cover a short distance. And if these negative states of consciousness did not reign over the minds and hearts of the overwhelming majority of the incarnated individuals, their influence could be neglected. The problem is that the so-called mass consciousness is prevailing in your world. And at this stage of human development, this mass consciousness becomes dangerous for the future destiny of the world. Therefore, you are given advice on how to get out of the influence of mass consciousness.

Only by giving preference to the contemplation of eternity unfolding in your hearts, is it possible to get rid of the negative energies that are so widespread in your society.

Changes are inevitable because they are caused by the rise of the vibrations of the planet as a whole. The more humanity will defend the old way of life and the former stereotypes of behavior supported by mass consciousness and by the negative impact of the majority of the media, including the Internet, the more severe tests humankind may undergo in the near future. Conversely, if qualitative changes take place in the consciousness of people, such as a leap of consciousness toward the Divinity, then the more smoothly the changes will take place.

It remains only to wait for the path humankind will choose this time. Many times in previous eras I had been incarnated on Earth during the most severe trials that humankind went through. And I was not the only one; there were many other Beings of Light. Now I come indirectly, using the conductors of our Messenger. But the value of my advice and directions does not become less significant because of that.

All of you will have to make your final choice in the near future about which path to follow: the Divine Path or continue manifesting your will in sticking to the path that leads nowhere.

It has never been told so clearly and concretely. I have come and I have warned you once again. Is it for the last time?

I AM Quan Yin,
with deep mercy and compassion
for your souls.

Mystical moment

Mystical moment

**I AM THAT I AM,
December 31, 2011**

I AM THAT I AM. And I come from within you.

Now, when one annual cycle has come to an end and another cycle is coming, it is time to think about the eternal.

The mystical moment of the change of the year and of the change of the epochs is coming.

It does not mean that the epoch is changing right at this moment. It means that the moment of eternity, when the change of the epochs occurs, has come.

At this moment it is necessary as never before to turn your eyes toward the eternal, the everlasting, the mystical, and the mysterious.

Now there are very few people who feel the Higher worlds. The sense of eternity is a gift that a person cannot attain within one incarnation. And the more people in embodiment who possess this gift — to feel the Higher worlds — the more harmonious are all the events of the physical world.

For, it is exactly the inner connection, a mystical connection, that opens within your being, that allows you to carry out the Divine changes in your world.

Neither governments nor countries nor individuals carry out the great transformations in the world. All the great transformations of the world have always taken place through the penetration of the higher energies into the world. And then, when the energies of the Higher worlds can penetrate into the physical world, everything starts changing very quickly, literally before your eyes.

Now we are on the cusp of the time and the age when the integration of the worlds will take place within more and more human individuals who are in embodiment.

The task, the purpose, and the meaning of life for many life-streams are exactly to hold and to maintain in their consciousness the connection with the Higher worlds, the connection between the worlds.

Then, when a sufficient number of human individuals are able to ascend to the Higher worlds in their consciousness, all the transformations, the Divine transformations of the world, take place.

Therefore, I insist that each of you finds the time in order to have your own mystical experience, your mystical experiment.

You must find the time to think about the eternal and the transitory, about eternal values and momentary interests, and to feel the difference between them and understand in which direction you wish to move.

At present, each person who is capable of mystical experience is considered strange and not adapted to life. However, this will not last forever. More and more human individuals, who keep the memory of the Higher worlds in their consciousness, will come into embodiment. And very soon these individuals will dominate the world. For the time has come. The time has come and space is changing. The worlds have become nearer and are ready for interpenetration.

When the illusion is in its last convulsions and tries to hold its positions, it is timely for me to remind you about your Divine origin and about the inner essence that is present within you that will not allow you to continue your sweet dream in the illusion.

It is time to awaken to the Higher reality. The time has come.

You are slow and do not wish to awaken from your sweet dreams in the illusion. However, the power and beauty of the Divine reality surpasses any of the best manifestations of your physical world.

Therefore, aspire to your true nature, your Divine nature. Look for these quiet mystical signs within yourselves. And then, when you become attuned to the Higher reality, the transformation of the physical world will happen by itself.

Do you see many people around you who think about the Higher reality and who are attuned to the Higher reality?

I think that there are not many. There are few of such people in embodiment. And this is the reason for any injustice that exists in your world, for any inharmonious manifestations of natural phenomena and mass riots in human society.

The reversal of your consciousness, centering on eternal values — humanity is now on the threshold of this stage of human evolution.

You need to realize the simple truth that you are now standing on this threshold, and just allow the existence of the Higher reality in your consciousness.

This will be the necessary and sufficient step that will enable the transformation of everything around you.

The Ascended Hosts are ready to help you. But in order for this help to be rendered, it is necessary for you to believe in the reality in which the Ascended Hosts exist. The Faith in the Higher reality and the aspiration to the Higher worlds can pull humanity out of sweet dreaming in the illusion.

The time to awaken has come.

The sun of the eternal reality is rising.

I call you to this everlasting reality. Now.

I AM THAT I AM.

Tatyana N. Mickushina

HOW TO AVOID CATACLYSMS

Please, leave your review about this book at amazon. com. This will greatly help in spreading the Teaching of the Ascended Masters given through the Messenger Tatyana Mickushina.

Websites:
http://sirius-eng.net (English version)
http://sirius-ru.net (Russian version)

Books by T.N.Mickushina on amazon.com:
amazon.com/author/tatyana_mickushina

Made in the USA
Las Vegas, NV
06 February 2023

67000453R00107